We're not alone. All across the country, in every city and in every town, folks like you and me are investing our hearts and dollars into maintaining or restoring historic neighborhoods. They are what I call urban pioneers, who rescue a neglected or abused home; others just love old homes and want to **preserve them.**

COMPANION

TO THE PUBLIC

TELEVISION

SERIES

ABOUT YOUR HOUSE

WITH **BOB YAPP**

To Roy!
Bob Yapp 6-12-99

BY **BOB YAPP** AND **RICH BINSACCA**

Production of the public television series *About Your House with Bob Yapp* is made possible by grants from ACE HARDWARE, ANDERSEN WINDOWS and THE NATIONAL TRUST FOR HISTORIC PRESERVATION.

BAY BOOKS

Bay Books & Tapes
555 De Haro St., No. 220
San Francisco, CA 94107.

Publisher: James Connolly
Editorial Director: Pamela Byers
Art Director: Jeffrey O'Rourke
Project Manager: Robert J. Dolezal
Editor: Louise Damberg
Project Editor: Barbara Dolezal
Book Design: Cabra Diseño/Tom Sieu
Photography: Alan Copeland & John Rickard
Illustrations: Ron Hildebrand
Photographs of Bob Yapp: Michael J. Winter

Educational and nonprofit groups wishing
to order this book at attractive quantity discounts may contact Bay Books & Tapes,
555 De Haro St., No. 220, San Francisco,
CA 94107.

Library of Congress Cataloguing-in-
Publication Data
Yapp, Bob.
    About your house with Bob Yapp /
Bob Yapp, Richard Binsacca
        p.   cm.
    "Companion to the Public Television
series."
    Includes index.
    ISBN 0-912333-38-3 (pbk.)
    1. Dwellings--Maintenance and repair.
2. Historic buildings--Conservation and
restoration.   I. Binsacca, Richard.
II. About your house with Bob Yapp
(Television program)   III. Title.
TH4817.Y37   1997
643'.7--dc21   97-36265
                     CIP

ISBN 0-912333-38-3

Manufactured in China

10 9 8 7 6 5 4 3 2 1

Distributed to the trade by
Publishers Group West

About Your House with Bob Yapp

dedication & thanks

This book is dedicated to my absolutely **incredible wife, Pat.** She has not only helped me raise our two wonderful kids, Nate and Megan, but she has done it while working a full-time career, with enthusiasm and love. She has supported this effort in more ways than I can say. She is my wife, my best friend, my partner, my devil's advocate, mother to my children and my co-conspirator.

Many thanks to my parents, for always believing in my abilities without question; Betty Hyde, my high school vice principal, who, despite my wild tendencies, believed in me; Bob Krebsbach, who taught me the value of craftsmanship; Van Harden, for giving me the chance to share my views on radio; Joe Lentz, whose enthusiasm and understanding kept me on the radio and put me on TV; Jim Egan, for teaching me to never give up; Bob Vila, without whom I would not be where I am today; Bruce Marcus, my co-executive producer and agent, who took a local hick and helped make him into a national hick; my sister Becky Powell, for dropping everything to help me with the show; my sister Sally Yapp Lehmann — if she were still alive, she would be amazed; Charles Yapp, my brother; Tim Ward, my director, for all his skills and listening abilities; Phil Douglas, my friend and keeper of my old houses; WHYY, Philadelphia, for helping get my pilot on PBS Pledge; WTTW, Chicago, for being a good partner in the series; Ace Hardware, Andersen Windows and the National Trust for Historic Preservation, for underwriting our first season and believing in the concept; and Bay Books and Tapes, for helping me write this book when I had no time to do it.

PRESERVING OUR HOMES
INTRODUCTION

TABLE OF
contents

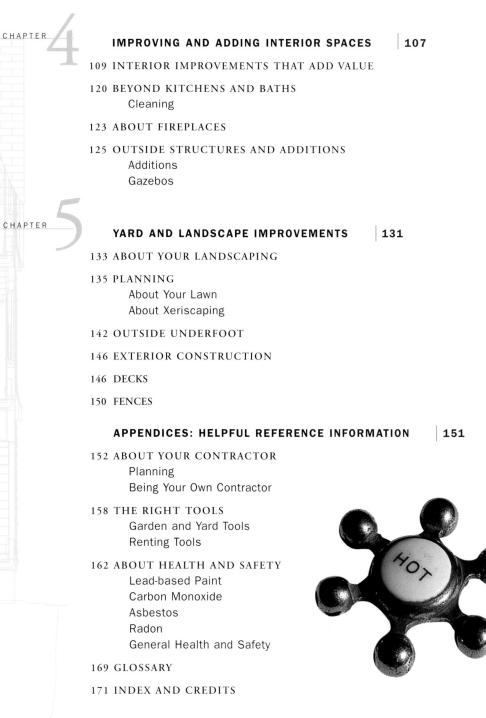

preserving our homes

A message from the National Trust for Historic Preservation

The National Trust for Historic Preservation provides underwriting support for *About Your House with Bob Yapp* as part of its continuing effort to help Americans bring preservation home. More than a how-to program, *About Your House with Bob Yapp* presents a practical approach to an important "why-to" message: why it's important to maintain your home and protect your investment and why embracing the places of America's past is a formula for success in the future.

People who love, maintain or restore old houses are practicing preservation every day. The National Trust hopes its support of *About Your House with Bob Yapp* on PBS delivers the information and techniques you need to do it right.

• • •

The National Trust, chartered by Congress in 1949, is a nonprofit organization whose mission is to provide leadership, education and advocacy to save America's diverse historic places and revitalize its communities.

More than 270,000 members support the National Trust's role as the leading voice of the preservation movement. The organization's programs encompass downtown revitalization, support for state and local organizations, litigation, advocacy, tourism, growth management, rural preservation and more. It assists in coordinating the efforts of preservation groups nationwide, provides professional advice through conferences and seminars, administers grant and loan programs, and maintains and operates historic sites for public visitation.

NATIONAL TRUST
FOR HISTORIC PRESERVATION

THE PAST BUILDS THE FUTURE.

In addition to serving as the national information clearinghouse for preservation, the National Trust publishes a variety of media that offer individuals and organizations access to a wealth of resources for their personal and community needs, including the award-winning *Preservation* Magazine (received free by all NTHP members), "Information" Series booklets, the *Historic Preservation Forum* professional journal, *Preservation Law Reporter*, a website with fee-based database services, and books and periodicals from Preservation Press (published by John Wiley & Sons, Inc., New York) and other publishers.

• • •

Preservation begins at home — in the houses we grew up in, the neighborhoods we build for ourselves and the communities we create for the next generation. It's about protecting what's here today while shaping what will live on tomorrow.

When you join the National Trust you help make preservation happen. For information on membership in the National Trust, its programs and services, call (800) 944-NTHP [(800) 944-6847]; visit the National Trust's website at www.nationaltrust.org, or write to: the National Trust for Historic Preservation, 1785 Massachusetts Avenue, NW, Washington, DC 20036, Att'n: About Your House.

introduction

The most vivid memories from my childhood are working with my dad on our Arts & Crafts home in Des Moines, Iowa.

When I sit back and reflect on why I got into this line of work in the first place, it always comes back to the fact that I prefer to do those things that I like doing best.

He bought this large family house in an excellent neighborhood because it was "the dog on the block," and although he was a corporate executive, he spent all of his free time renovating it. One of my main jobs was to stand on a ladder, holding up drywall with my head, as he nailed it. He also had a wood-working shop in the basement and let me use and abuse most all of his tools.

My mother was a writer and an antiques dealer, so I was surrounded by creativity, renovation and history throughout my childhood. Mom always gave my brother, sisters and me the same advice: "Do what you love, work hard and smart, become an expert and pass your knowledge on to others. Don't worry about 'the money'; if you do what you love, you will make a living." For all four of us, this advice has been true from the get-go. It has allowed us to have fun and, I believe, lead interesting lives.

In high school I begged my way into an apprenticeship with a furniture and cabinetmaker from "the old school." He wouldn't let me use anything electric the first year. His attitude was that you first learn about wood and how to work it by hand. As a kid I was disgusted with this — I wanted to use power tools, but it didn't take long to figure out that learning to cut hand dovetails and mortise and tenon joints was giving me an invaluable appreciation for quality craftsmanship, and it has served me ever since.

In college I studied construction management and history. But, although I wanted to, apprentice with an historic preservation contractor, I couldn't — there just weren't any. After working for several general contractors, it became apparent I needed to buy an old house and figure out how to restore it myself. A partner and I bought a two-story Craftsman-style home. We learned a lot the hard way restoring that house. I read the limited selection of books on the subject and discovered a heavy-duty newsletter called the *Old House Journal.* (By the way, this newsletter is now a full-blown magazine you should read.)

Since those times I have had the pleasure of designing and building hundreds of pieces of furniture and being involved in the restoration and renovation of more than 130 historic homes.

In 1988 I began thinking about my mom's advice to share what I'd learned and began writing a weekly column in the *Des Moines Register* and then the *Quad City Times* called "The House Doctor." At the same time, I started writing for some national magazines. Based on the incredible number of letters received from readers, it became apparent that people were hungry for information about taking care of their old homes without messing up the historic character of these houses. I soon began a weekly radio show on Saturdays. The response blew me away. It wasn't long before it was syndicated and we were really getting the info out to the public.

By that time I felt my listeners would appreciate a more visual medium. I went to Joe Lentz, the CEO of the radio network, and suggested we produce a video targeted to my radio listeners. Although I knew nothing about television production, I believed I had a pretty good handle on what these folks wanted to know and see. The one-hour program was called "The House Doctor: Top Ten Tips for a Healthy Home." Soon after the video came out I met Bruce Marcus, a producer working primarily with PBS programming. He understood the potential and convinced PBS Pledge to offer the program as a special. It aired successfully during 1995 and 1996 in multiple markets around the country.

Today I give a lot of talks and seminars nationwide to all kinds of groups of old-house owners. The title is usually "Preservation Doesn't Cost, It Pays." When I first began doing this I figured the attendees would be small groups of hard-core preservationists. Boy, was I wrong. I was astounded by the numbers and the types of folks who showed up. Factory workers, hog farmers, urban pioneers, lawyers, truck drivers, accountants, homemakers — in other words, just about anyone you could imagine. These folks, to the person, want quality information on how to take care of, restore, renovate and maintain their old houses. They want to do the right thing to preserve the integrity of these homes, but they feel left out.

Mainstream America has been left out of the preservation movement, and that is a mistake, but there are many who care about our architectural heritage. If society as a whole would think more in these terms, we wouldn't have to restore or renovate our houses because they would be properly maintained from the start.

But the sad truth is, we've become a throwaway society, more willing to choke our landfills by as much as 40 percent with construction and demolition debris to immediately gratify our desire for new, expensive and substandardly built homes with three-car garages.

Don't get me wrong: there are lots of creative and innovative new construction techniques and technologies out there, and we should use them. But, as I drive through new housing developments, I see that many of the insights gained from thousands of years of building knowledge have been thrown out for the sake of expediency. These cornfield developments will become, in short time, our future slums. Our great grandchildren will have to tear them down because they were built so badly. But older houses in historic old neighborhoods generally were built for the future, as long as we maintain them.

My primary goals in producing my TV program and writing this book are simple and straightforward:

- To promote the preservation of America's old and historic homes.

- To provide a quality standard you should expect when having any work done on your home, old or new.

- To disseminate basic information on how things should be done, so you'll know the right questions to ask.

- To lend affordable ideas for maintaining your home.

- To show how to do many things yourself.

This book is a companion to my PBS television series, *About Your House with Bob Yapp*. You will find many of the subjects covered on the show within these pages for easy referral. We organized the book into five chapters. Chapter One discusses the benefits of owning an older home and how preservation pays you as well as your community and the environment. Subsequent chapters talk about how to restore the exterior and interior of your home to museum quality affordably while accommodating modern conveniences, how to improve and add on to your home without sacrificing its historical integrity and how to renovate your yard and garden to maintain the style and character of your house.

We've also included appendices on hiring a contractor, the government's official guidelines for historic restoration and the tools you should have to maintain your property once the restoration work is done. Finally, our glossary of terms will guide you through the nomenclature of home renovation.

Shooting 26 half-hour programs per year and producing this book turned out to be a much bigger job than I imagined, but in every way they have fulfilled my parents' legacy. While the information we're imparting to you in these pages is serious, we hope we've presented it in a format that is entertaining, informative and user-friendly.

Thanks for taking the time to read my book.

BOB YAPP

There's a neighborhood in your town that you go out of your way to drive through on your way to work. The one that has **big, old trees** with gnarled trunks and branches that canopy over the street. Where the homes are set back far from the curb and narrow alleys lead to the garages and carports tucked behind them. Mail is delivered on foot, to the door, not to a box at the curb. The homes themselves provide a lesson in American architecture; on one street you might pass a Georgian next to a Craftsman bungalow across the street from an Italianate two doors down from a Frank Lloyd Wright.

You don't live in this neighborhood, but you wish you did. If you grew up in the same town, you've watched folks restore "the dog" on the block, inspired by the

There's nothing more exciting to see than a beautifully maintained neighborhood of historic homes.

care their neighbors have taken to maintain the character and history of their own homes and therefore the whole neighborhood. You admire the neighborhood's integration of various cultures and people, its proximity to quaint corner markets and local eateries, and its everyday vitality. You promise yourself you'll check into buying the next home that posts a "for sale" sign on its front lawn. You're my kind of people, driven by a passion for preserving the past.

We're not alone; all across the country, in every city, folks like you and me are investing our hearts and dollars into maintaining or restoring these neighborhoods. Some are what I call urban pioneers, who rescue a neglected or abused home; others just love old homes and want to preserve them.

Not that we're impractical about our passion. For instance, I may advocate the restoration of a museum-quality exterior for an older home, but I also recognize the demand to make it livable and convenient for a modern family lifestyle. I've learned you can accomplish both objectives, and it's cheaper than buying a new, modern home or tearing down an older home and rebuilding.

It's no surprise to me that preservation and restoration is the fastest-growing segment of the home construction industry. Simply, preservation pays. It pays financially, in that it is cheaper in the long run to repair, restore and maintain an older home than purchase a new one and frequently yields dramatic returns upon appraisal or resale. It pays emotionally; you become a part of living history while adding your own stamp to the home's character. It pays the community, which benefits from a visual legacy of its architectural history. It pays the

Despite its obvious neglect, this historic home exhibits all of the interesting features that will make it a treasure after it is renovated to like-new condition.

FOLLOWING PAGE
The dining room of Lyndhurst (1838), a National Trust for Historic Preservation historical site in Tarrytown, New York, reflects its status as the finest surviving Gothic Revival mansion in America. The pointed arch and leaded-glass windows showcase the ornate furnishings.

environment, by utilizing recycled and remanufactured materials; whereas new home construction contributes up to half of the waste in our landfills.

Salvaging the past I don't believe that homes have a natural life span. Homes and neighborhoods in Europe and Asia have been standing for centuries and not just because the homes are made out of stone and brick instead of wood. Any house can be restored and lived in for hundreds of years or more if enough care is taken to maintain it properly.

Yet tens of thousands of homes a year are destroyed in this country, some by nature but most by man, perhaps even rightly so if they otherwise could not be saved and were unsafe to occupy. But those leveled in the name of progress are lost forever, removing a piece of history and dumping an estimated 5 pounds or more per square foot into our already overflowing landfills.

Old-house recycling isn't just about preserving the whole, though. History can live on if the significant pieces from a dilapidated structure can be salvaged and reused to restore original character to a home next door, elsewhere in town or even across the country. Likewise, a restoration project may stall or be shelved if an older, neglected home has been pilfered of its architectural details. I call this "urban mining," and I liken it to robbing a jewelry store. That's why I recommend mothballing older homes (as opposed to tearing them down completely) to protect their contents for future restoration projects; if a home is beyond saving, I can only hope the salvaged elements are removed by someone — or some organization — that cares.

Many landfills contain the shattered remains of homes that might have been salvaged along with their contents.

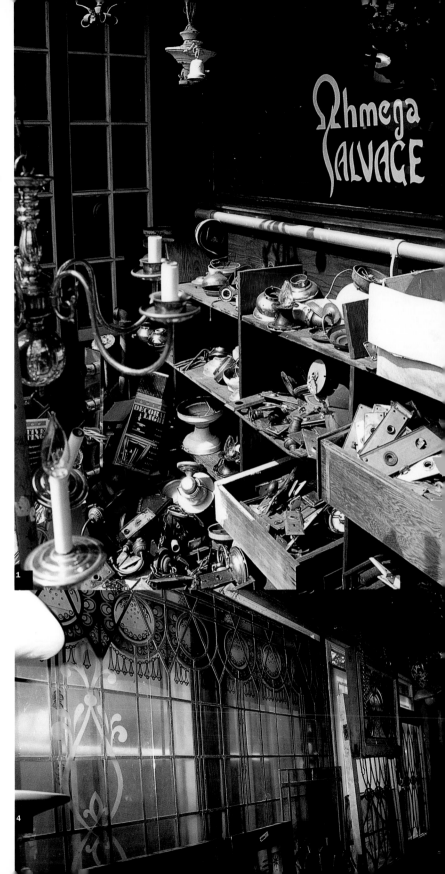

1 Most larger communities have antiques stores and salvage yards filled with architectural details and fixtures salvaged by careful demolition of homes beyond repair.

2 Clawfoot bathtubs and pedestal sinks, even in rough condition, are easy to restore at a lower cost than buying new fixtures.

3 Antique lighting fixtures — often with one-of-a-kind features — abound in salvage yards. Refinishing and rewiring them is easily arranged through expert craftsmen.

4 Among the many beautiful restoration items that may be incorporated into one's home, stained and leaded-glass panels provide the biggest bang for the buck.

5 Window moldings and gingerbread details gathered from old houses during demolition can find new life in your home.

Fortunately, what began 20 years ago as a cottage industry of folks like me simply trying to preserve history has grown into a full-fledged, multimillion-dollar business of high-quality salvage shops, period restoration suppliers and remanufacturers. Just check out the classified section of any home improvement magazine and you'll find it filled with ads for these businesses.

Searching salvage outlets for period pieces that are appropriate for your "new" older home requires a bit of knowledge. The best way to find out what materials and products belong in your home is to investigate and document its history properly. Start by reviewing records kept at the nearest building department or deed office and reading local history books about town founders, cultural influences and historic neighborhoods and structures. You want to pinpoint as nearly as possible when the home was originally built, as well as date any additions such as a porch or garage.

No matter the style of a house I'm restoring, I'm always on the lookout for old, freestanding claw-and-ball bathtubs and interesting sinks. Even those with some rust or stains are prime candidates for restoration and are much less expensive to rehab than purchase new. Quality door hardware, as long as it can be salvaged in near-complete sets and is free of corrosion, is always a good find.

Lighting fixtures, even those from the gas and oil days, are timeless; if you can acquire their shades and bulbs, all the better. And old-style panel doors, because of their construction, can often be restored to their original condition and appearance.

One of my favorite projects is rescuing and restoring a soaking tub, then installing a Victorian-era shower ring and fitting around it. Such a project not only enhances the interior design and decor of a bathroom, but it costs about one-third the price of a new tub-and-shower assembly. Sometimes all it takes is a wire brush to remove the rust on the underside and a good-quality cleaner to shine up the tub basin.

If the tub isn't in good shape, with rust pervading the underside and sections of the basin chipped or missing, there's likely a restoration shop nearby that can sandblast off the rust and reenamel the basin for only a few hundred dollars — a pittance compared to buying a new claw-and-ball tub. The shop may even be able to do the work at your home. Typical enamel refinishing takes a few days to cure, or dry, before you can attach fixtures and fittings and connect the plumbing lines, but it's well worth the wait.

Molly

Brown house

This Queen Anne house, a Denver landmark listed on the National Register of Historic Places, is best known as the home of the "unsinkable" Molly Brown. Its distinctive detailing reflects the taste and image of its former owner.

About architectural investigation

The Secretary of the Interior's Preservation Brief #35 outlines the four basic steps of architectural investigation: historic research, documentation, inventory and stabilization.

The first step includes research of visual, oral and written history that can provide some valuable information about the structure and the property. Deeds, permits, construction documents (plans and specifications), as well as family albums and other memorabilia can help determine a sequence of ownership and chronology of changes or additions to the house. Most old houses, especially those older than 75 years, have probably gone through several stages of change to accommodate new technologies, changing lifestyles, matters of convenience

and solutions to chronic maintenance or systems problems.

The documentation process is best done with a still or video camera, the latter of which must remain fixed on each detail long enough to document its features properly. The advantage of video, of course, is that you can narrate what you're seeing, then easily transfer that information to a floor plan or model of the house as you get more involved in the restoration of its various architectural features and elements. You'll also want to get some establishing shots to show how the house is oriented on the property and what its dominant landscape features are.

Next step: inventory. As with the homework required for salvaged materials, this task requires a careful accounting of the various elements and details that offer clues to your

home's history. Even if a detail appears out of place for the period or style of architecture, it should be documented and preserved for future study or use elsewhere.

Finally, stabilization pertains to any hazardous or dilapidated structural elements that could cause major damage, render the house unfit for occupancy or hinder the restoration or preservation process. These conditions might dictate repairing the roof or gutter system, covering gaps in the sidewalls or windows, or shoring up porch columns or structural beams.

Also included in Preservation Brief #35's dozen pages are detailed instructions for high-tech testing and analysis of a home's materials and systems; for the lay person, it provides a heads-up regarding the proper steps to take to accomplish these tests.

Buying an older house Buying an older or historic home is nothing to fear; like anything else, if you know, understand and follow the right steps in the proper order, you'll be, well, home-free. To make an informed decision, you'll need to weigh the time, money, effort and anxiety you'll expend throughout the job against the value of such an investment.

The Office of Historic Preservation in Washington, D.C., among other state and local offices dedicated to the preservation of historic structures and resources, offers a wealth of information about finding, investigating, documenting and restoring an older home. In fact, Preservation Brief #35 specifically addresses the process of architectural investigation in a comprehensive, step-by-step format. It also lays the groundwork for the Secretary of the Interior's Standards for the Treatment of Historic Properties [see pages 14 and 15], which must be followed if a house is to be considered for the National Register of Historic Places or similar state or local designation.

Once your investigative work is done, you'll want to get a professional home inspection. Some states and municipalities require them, and most at least encourage them before a sale is closed and ownership transferred. It's a good idea, for your protection as well as the seller's, who wants to limit his or her liability as much as possible for defects or other problems that should have been disclosed or repaired prior to the sale.

A quality home inspector is likely a former builder or tradesperson who has seen just about everything and is especially knowledgeable about local architectural

The first steps in purchasing an older home are the same as for any other property: lots of diligence in finding and inspecting the home for sale. Using a knowledgeable local real estate agent is a tremendous aid, and it costs the buyer nothing.

quirks. For a home that basically is in move-in condition, an inspector will check out the major systems of the house, testing their operation and assessing their overall condition. For a fee of about $200 or slightly more, an inspector will return a complete, system-by-system evaluation of the house and note items that are in need of immediate attention. This report is not only useful as a bargaining chip during the negotiation of the sale but also can serve as the basis for a restoration or preservation work estimate.

For homes that have been mothballed or must be restored prior to moving in, I tell folks to invest in the services of a restoration consultant. For $500 to perhaps a few thousand dollars, a restoration consultant will deliver plans, specifications and a cost estimate to bring your home back to life. Unlike a contractor, however, he or she will not do the actual work; rather, along with an unbiased assessment of your home's condition, a restoration consultant can help you seek out a contractor to restore the home for occupancy.

You also should do your own inspection. Walk the neighborhood and take note of how the homes are maintained, both overall and individually. Are new, out-of scale homes sprouting up on infill lots where older homes used to stand, or has the area been revitalized with thoughtful restorations and historic preservation projects? In short, is this the type of neighborhood in which you want to live?

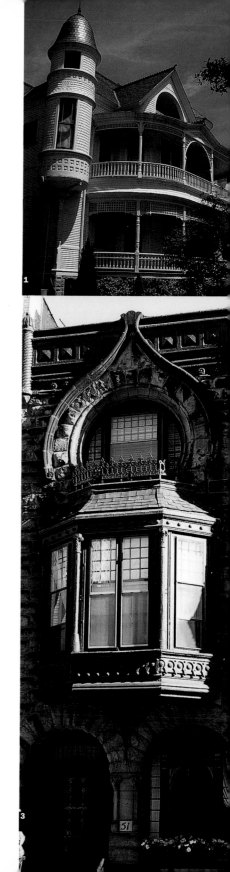

2

A short sampling of homes throughout America

1 **Sottile House, in Charleston, South Carolina, typifies the Queen Anne style. It is located on the historic campus of the College of Charleston.**

2 **Bremond House. This Second Empire–style home resides in Austin, Texas, in a block designated as a National Historical District.**

3 **This row house in Chicago, Illinois, is an exotic mixture of Richardson Romanesque and Moorish Revival styles captured by the builder and architect in this unnamed city dwelling.**

4 **Located in Cos Cob, Connecticut, a Second Empire roof adorns this early nineteenth-century classic.**

Federal Standards for Preservation The United States Secretary of the Interior publishes standards and guidelines for the preservation, rehabilitation, restoration and reconstruction of buildings, including homes. These four terms are distinct and carry their own set of rules, but they all are founded on maintaining our architectural and archeological history for future generations.

The guidelines are for serious home restorers and preservationists, not those looking to cash in on a quick real estate investment. Unless you receive federal money to restore or rehabilitate an older structure, these rules are enforced only by your commitment to historical preservation; officially, the guidelines pertain only to grant-in-aid projects assisted through the National

Historic Preservation Fund, but everyone should refer to them as they restore, rehabilitate, preserve or reconstruct an older home.

Listed below, straight out of the book, are the Secretary of the Interior's Standards for Rehabilitation, a list of ten tenets that guide me (and my own interpretation of each in layman's terms):

1. A property will be used as it was historically or be given a new use that requires minimal changes to its distinctive materials, features, spaces and spatial relationships. (In short, either use the structure as it was intended or preserve its character and general forms if you plan to use it in some other way.)

2. The historic character of a property will be retained and preserved. The removal of

distinctive materials or alteration of features, spaces and spatial relationships that characterize a property will be avoided. (Underscores the previous item by protecting historic features.)

3. Each property will be recognized as a physical record of its time, place and use. Changes that create a false sense of historical development, such as adding a conjectural feature or elements from other historic properties, will not be undertaken. (Don't try to re-create history; let it stand on its own.)

4. Changes to a property that have acquired historic significance in their own right will be retained and preserved. (Clear enough with respect to the home's evolution as a family shelter.)

5. Distinctive materials, features, finishes and

construction techniques or examples of craftsmanship that characterize a property will be preserved. (Translation: Leave the original plaster mold and hand-crafted mantelpiece where they are.)

6. Deteriorated historic features will be repaired rather than replaced. Where the severity of deterioration requires replacement of a distinctive feature, the new feature will match the old in design, color, texture and, where possible, materials. Replacement of missing features will be substantiated by documentary and physical evidence. (Hence the growth of restoration shops, salvage businesses and period re-creation outlets. And save what can't be restored, just in case someone wants to know.)

7. Chemical or physical treatments, if appropriate, will be undertaken using the gentlest means possible. Treatments that cause damage to historic materials will not be used. (As you will discover in subsequent chapters, this is why I recommend gentle strippers and cleaners rather than sandblasting or high-pressure washing.)

8. Archeological resources will be protected and preserved in place. If such resources must be disturbed, mitigation measures will be taken. (Outbuildings, stone walls and even outhouses have historic value; just make sure if you discover a family burial site or other sacred ground that you hire a professional to replace it properly elsewhere and document its contents, or, find ways to work around it.)

9. New additions, exterior alterations or related new construction will not destroy historic materials, features or spatial relationships that characterize the property. The new work will be differentiated from the old and will be compatible with the historic materials, features, size, scale and proportion, and massing to protect the integrity of the property and its environment. (Don't make an addition look like it has been there from the beginning; construct it so that future generations will easily recognize its place in time or be able to remove it from the original, undamaged structure.)

10. New additions and adjacent or related new construction will be undertaken in such a manner that, if removed in the future, the essential form and integrity of the historic property and its environment would be unimpaired. (As you will hear in the coming pages many times: "Do No Harm").

Go back to the house you're considering and peer between the shrubs and the foundation to get a sense of the drainage pattern. Check the condition of the paved areas — pathways, a patio and the driveway. Note the number and condition of downspout extenders and the fitness of the sidewall paint and roof. Inspect the window sills for peeling or cracking paint. And make sure to write down what you see, hear and uncover so you can use it down the road; it will prove to be important information at closing or during your preservation project.

Next comes the appraisal process, which will determine the fair market value of the home and property relative to the surrounding neighborhood or community. An appraiser, typically from or hired by the lending institution considering your mortgage loan, should consider "comps," or nearby houses with similar features, footage and number of rooms as a key indicator of your home's value. But with that, an appraiser should factor in the direction the neighborhood is taking and how the value of your property will be affected. You can help by providing your appraiser or lender with any blueprints, specifications and cost estimates relating to restoration work planned for the house. The value of future work will be accounted for in the overall appraisal and loan approval process.

1 Home inspection begins with a careful look at every exposed feature of the prospective home. Here, the windows will require a complete renovation to restore their original function and beauty.

2 Beneath-the-surface defects are identified during professional inspections: pest, roof, structural and general home. Termites and other insect pests sometimes can be eliminated by tenting the home and injecting poison gas.

3 Major appliances included in the sale should be evaluted for safety and function by a professional. Many utilities offer low- or no-cost inspections to protect customers from hazards.

4 Filling out the blanks on a real estate loan application is the first of hundreds of pieces of paper executed during a real estate transaction.

5 The home stretch begins when moving-in day arrives.

6 The satisfaction of a newly acquired old house — whether in the city or the country — is evident to the entire neighborhood.

Once you're approved for the loan and the day of closing is near, make a final walk-through of the house with your real estate agent, noting anything that has changed since the original inspections were performed. No doubt you've walked through the home several times before, but this time tour with your inspection or renovation report in hand to be sure all the items that were there before are still in place and all fixtures and systems still work. Depending on the nature of the items discovered, you may be able to require that the seller make repairs as a condition of closing the sale.

During your walk-through, turn on the lights, test the thermostat (both heating and cooling modes), run the faucets and flush the toilets to test the water pressure, and check the number and placement of electrical outlets. Fire up the stove and any other appliances included in the sale; check the condition of the floors, walls and ceilings for water damage, sagging or buckling to make sure you're not walking into a project that's more than you expected. It's your last opportunity to assure that your dream home will be just that.

CHAPTER two:

THE HOME exterior

An architect friend put it best when he said that **builders** in the early part of this century asked first what looks good from the outside and made the interior spaces work within that aesthetic. This way of thinking created homes that featured remarkable attention to the exterior materials and detailing; it also married the contours and features of the building to its site and natural surroundings and directed the functional layout of the interior spaces, creating the curious and charming interior nooks and crannies we treasure in older homes. (As architects began to install Victorian-era stylings, interiors received just as much attention as the exterior of the home.)

The thinking behind today's subdivision tract housing seems just the opposite. Many new and remodeled homes are designed or redesigned from the inside out, with the exterior a secondary consideration. We've made the car and the TV priorities, and built or added spaces to accommodate them, sometimes, it seems, with little regard for how the outside looks.

From its foundation to its roof, your home's exterior defines its character and style and defends it against the hostile elements of the climate.

For this reason, anyone who knows me or has seen my show or read my newsletter knows I'm not a big fan of the new, mass-market construction and remodeling industries — which is not to say that all builders and contractors today put up junk. In some cases, I've seen dramatic interior changes and even additions to older homes that maintained their historic appeal and the appearance of their facades (discussed further in Chapter Four). And I have no problem (generally) with the architect-designed and custom-built homes of today, some of which are thoughtful of past traditions or have broken new architectural ground and will be historically significant in the future.

But by and large, as I travel through older (and newer) neighborhoods, I can't help but cringe at some of the things I see: vinyl siding on a Victorian, three layers of asphalt comp shingles piled on top of each other, a misplaced addition stuck onto the side of a Cape.

The exterior features of a house, even a new one, are what attracts us to it in the first place. The placement, integration and detailing of the windows and doors, porches and balconies, bump-outs and drip edges, not to mention the materials used for these elements, create a home's character.

So, as you contemplate restoring, repairing and preserving your older home, I urge you to hark back to the philosophy of the past and respect the design and materials that are original and appropriate to its exterior. With that directive in mind, this chapter discusses the three key elements of your home's exterior: the

Early home builders and architects knew what they were doing — inside and out. Starting with the visual impact of the home, they defined its spaces and structure to create a dwelling that fit the family's needs.

roof, siding and foundation. We'll delve into everything from materials choices and installation and maintenance to potential problems and fixes. You'll gain insight into a home exterior's biggest challenge (water) and what I call the Big Lie about replacement siding, among other helpful revelations. I hope the information inspires you to remain true to your home's history while helping you achieve that goal within your budget.

Roofs and eaves Let's take it from the top. Your roof is your home's first defense against the elements and a key component of its architectural history and aesthetic character. For better or worse, you can dramatically change the look of an old house simply by altering the roof's original material.

American housing features several types of roof forms, each inspired and adapted from historic models and typically derived from the architect's or builder's heritage and the overall house design. (The roof material was selected in much the same way, as well as for the home's proximity to the source of various raw materials, such as timber and stone.)

In the Midwest, we enjoy a wide diversity of home styles featuring a variety of roof forms that commonly are finished with cedar shingles (given our proximity to vast timber baskets). Homes along the East Coast are more formal in design, featuring long, straight rooflines with slate roofing from nearby quarries. Houses along the Sunbelt feature low-sloping roofs with clay tiles, given the influence of Spanish and Mediterranean architecture and building practices.

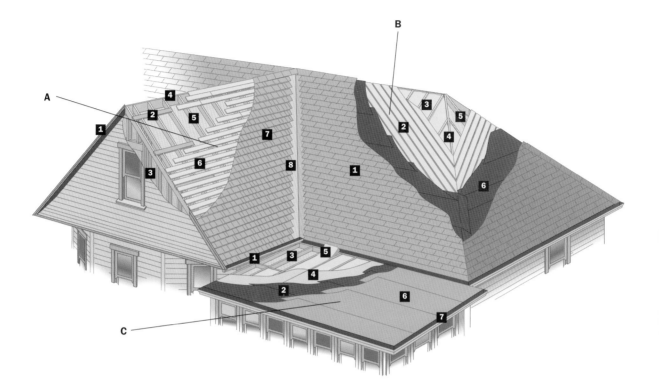

A Cedar Shingle on a Gable Roof

1 Drip edge on cornice

2 Lookout rafter supporting cornice and eaves

3 Exterior wall stud

4 Ridge board

5 Rafter

6 Spaced sheathing

7 Layered cedar shingles

8 Valley rafter with open metal flashing

B Original Composition Shingle on a Hip Roof

1 Composition shingle

2 Diagonally applied solid sheathing (also applied horizontally, or as plywood and composition panels)

3 Roll fiberglass insulation

4 Hip rafter

5 Jack rafter

6 Roofing felt construction paper

C Flat or Built-up Roof

1 Slope for water runoff to gutter system

2 Roofing felt construction paper

3 Roof joist

4 Solid composition or plywood board sheathing

5 Roll fiberglass insulation

6 Asphalt composition roll roofing

7 Gutter system

An interesting roofline is a prime factor in your overall house style. Shown here are two examples: a mansard-style roof (top) and a cottage with many gables and planes.

Roof forms are easy to identify once you know the terms. A pitched roof, for instance, is one with a distinctive slope from the peak (or ridge) to the eaves. Pitch is expressed in terms like 4-in-12, which means the roof elevates 4 inches for every 12 inches in length. Most older homes typically have steep, or high-pitched, roofs (8-in-12 or more), the result of historic architectural influences, interior space demands and climate.

Pitched roofs come in many styles, but the most common are gable and hipped [see illustration, previous page]. While some roofs, like those from the Victorian era, may feature bump-outs or other breaks in the roofline, they still should follow the main form, either gable or hipped, to maintain a consistent, clean look. Next time you drive by a house with a complicated roof design, featuring such elements as dormers, bump-outs, covered entries and the like, ask yourself whether it is gable or hipped — and if all the roof elements follow proper roof design, meaning they have the same general form and pitch.

Other roof forms, such as mansard, gambrel, shed and flat are less common, especially as the primary roof form of the house; still, you may see them used on adaptive reuse projects (like a barn or carriage house turned into living space) or an appropriate addition, like a second-story shed dormer.

You still can get almost any roofing material of the past, but they long-since have been supplemented by asphalt composition shingles (the most popular roofing today), various kinds of metals and even plastic and synthetics. These newer roofing materials, particularly asphalt composition shingles, can be manufactured to replicate wood or slate roofs of the past, offering a lightweight, faster-to-install alternative to a true replication job, which may be cost-prohibitive. Properly maintained, asphalt comp shingles will last upwards of 25 years, cost less initially than a wood shingle roof and be easy to repair if sections are damaged or torn off.

No matter what type of roofing material you choose, it is paramount that it be correctly flashed, fastened and finished to protect your home from the weather and ensure it lasts its expected life. To determine your roof's current condition and history, I suggest a two-stage inspection: from the ground and up close on a sturdy, well-supported ladder. From the ground, you'll be able to see signs of general wear, such as missing shingles, areas that are bald or discolored, or sections with a wave or sway in them. Depending on the extent of the wear, tear and disrepair, it may be clear even from that perspective that you need to completely replace your roof. But I still recommend an up-close inspection.

There's no need to climb up on the roof itself, which may be dangerously weak or slick. The view from eaves-level, a much safer spot, will tell you what you need to know. From there, you can see much more clearly how the roofing material has worn — upturned or brittle cedar shingles, missing granules on asphalt comp shingles or popped fasteners on metal.

This type of close inspection also will tell you how many layers of shingles are currently on the roof, providing a valuable history of the original roofing material and subsequent reroofing projects.

To examine your roof and its gutters or eaves, a sturdy extension ladder is an invaluable aid.

A tear-off, whether the roof is asphalt or wood shingle, reveals the structural underlay beneath the weatherproof outer layer: spaced sheathing.

Assuming your roof needs to be completely replaced (we'll get into partial replacements and repairs a little later in this chapter), I'm of the school that recommends a complete tear-off of all roofing material down to the sheathing, even if there's just one layer of roofing on the structure.

The reason? If your roof shows some damage or wear, it's probably due to a moisture problem, improper ventilation, incorrect flashing, a structural defect, infestation, or maybe the roof is simply past its effective life span. Whatever the reason, it will continue to deteriorate and likely affect the quality and life expectancy of the new material on top of it.

In addition to performance, there are other reasons not to cover up an existing roof with new material. Most important, it is nearly impossible to flash properly over or around an existing roof, and flashing is the key element for protecting a roof's most vulnerable areas from leaks due to water and snow runoff. In addition, your new roof likely will not lay flat with something in various stages of wear underneath it. Finally, you need to consider the weight that multiple layers will put on your roof's structure, few of which are engineered, even in today's high-tech world, to support more than a layer or two.

Simply put, if you're going to spend the money to get a quality roof, go all the way. Tear-offs usually cost an additional 15 percent or so, but they're worth it to uncover and fix problems and assure your new roof has a fair chance at a long life and looks its best.

Like most demolition work, a roof tear-off is usually fast and chaotic, with shingles, old nails, metal flashing and felt paper piling up on ground tarps for disposal. Depending on the condition, style and size of your roof, it shouldn't take more than a full day and a four-person crew to complete the tear-off and reveal the sheathing, the boards or panels that provide the surface to which your new shingles will be fastened.

If your house originally had a cedar shingle roof, chances are the tear-off will reveal a roof frame with slats that form a ladderlike deck along the entire length of the structural frame. Spaced about 3 to 5 inches apart and set perpendicular to the roof rafters, these slats (or spaced sheathing) measure about the same as today's 1x4 lumber. The slats allow the underside of cedar shingles to dry out after absorbing water during a rainfall or snowstorm. You'll want to repair or replace any damaged or missing slats before moving on (that is, unless you're planning to reroof with asphalt composition shingles or metal, in which case the sheathing should be solid; discussed later in this chapter).

As mentioned, the most critical step of any reroofing job is the flashing. The job of flashing is to protect areas on a roof that are the most vulnerable to water leakage — the valleys (where the downsides of two pitches intersect, creating a gutter to the eaves) and the various openings, such as vent pipes, chimneys and dormers. If there is a problem with a roof, most likely it is rooted in flashing that is worn away or was improperly installed.

Poor flashing around vents and chimneys permits leaks to develop. Metal flashings should be woven into both the mortar and the shingles.

An open valley with cut
sides and metal flashing
(top) usually is preferable to
a closed or woven valley
(bottom).

Because proper flashing is metal (of various kinds and gauges), it may still be in decent condition even if the roofing material needs to be replaced. While patching damaged sections of flashing can be problematic, it may be prudent and cost-effective to recycle what you can; a reputable roofer will know what to save and restore and what to throw away.

There are generally two ways to flash a valley: closed (also called woven or cut) and open. With a closed or woven system, the roofing material itself acts as the flashing; sections are interlocked (or woven) to create a seamless appearance. This technique requires the roofer to cut the material so it will weave together properly, but I think this creates an inherent defect in the shingle and leads to a higher likelihood of water leakage.

I much prefer open flashing, in which a continuous, molded piece of metal creates a seam between the roofing material and the area being protected (be it a chimney or a valley). Open flashing is easier to install properly and remains accessible for repairing worn or damaged sections. It relieves the roofing material from bearing the brunt of water saturation, and, as mentioned, some metal flashing can outlast the roof material.

Metal flashing is available in a wide range of finishes and quality. (Notice I didn't mention tar as a flashing alternative, a topic I reserve for special discussion). The most common today is bright aluminum, typically of lightweight, 26-gauge stock, which makes up in cost-efficiency and durability what it may lack in aesthetic quality. Aluminum, however, should not be used to flash around a chimney because it reacts with the mortar, causing the metal to deteriorate prematurely. If you're averse to its bright contrast to your selection of roofing material, there are a few time-tested alternatives.

Galvanized (or zinc-coated) metal is the next most common flashing material and is available at a comparable price and in similar gauges as aluminum. It is easily worked around protrusions, peaks and valleys; its Achilles' heel is that it doesn't hold paint very effectively, requiring periodic maintenance.

Another common flashing material, especially on those old Colonials and coastal area homes of the Northeast and Atlantic states, is lead. Durable and able to be seamlessly shaped and molded around various protrusions, lead is still common on these homes and is often reused on reroofing jobs because of its stamina. Aesthetically, its dull color also blends well with a variety of roofing materials.

Even more widely used is copper, for both aesthetic and practical reasons. It is beautiful (weathering to a rich green patina), can be bent into any shape and, with proper maintenance, can last literally hundreds of years. Its main downside: cost. Today, copper's high price is the single most important reason the material generally is used to accent only a smaller covered area, such as over a bay window, rather than for an entire roof.

Finally, there is terne flashing, a tin/lead coating over an iron base. Terne was a common enough roofing material in the late 1800s but required more maintenance than wood, slate or asphalt composition roofing. As flashing, it is economically comparable to aluminum in some areas (though it is more

Bucket o' tar **The Uniform Building Code (UBC), which has been adopted by most of the Western and Midwestern states, sets the minimum standards by which homes and other structures are built. The UBC doesn't specify a particular method or material for flashing but rather just requires it for all vertical protrusions through a roof. Still, any roofer worth his salt and your money would never resort to black tar as a suitable flashing material. Not only is it messy and careless, it quickly dries and cracks, eliminating any value as a protector against water leaks. (Truth be known, most local building inspectors will only approve metal for flashing.) So if your roofer shows up with a bucket of tar, send him packing. I guarantee you it will never perform as well as a quality metal flashing job and is probably indicative of your roofer's overall skills — that is, sloppy, fast and dull.**

difficult to obtain and therefore more expensive in others) and typically is installed as a standing seam or interlocking panel system. It lasts longer if painted as part of your annual maintenance regimen.

Whatever flashing material you choose, keep in mind a few installation tips: First, wherever possible, flashing should be installed in continuous, single-piece lengths, thus reducing the number of joints (or openings and overlaps) that will need to be sealed against the elements. Also, have a crimp (or seam) installed along the length of the deepest part of the valley flashing (referred to by roofers as "W-valley flashing"), which will inhibit water from splashing under the shingles.

Second, familiarize yourself with such terms as "step" and "counter" flashing, which are especially relevant when flashing around a chimney or an addition. Step flashing, which gets its name from the way the metal pieces are stepped up the sides of the wall or chimney, consists of single pieces of metal bent to the proper angle and slope and installed along intersecting vertical walls and under each course of shingles.

Counter flashing, similar in size to step flashing, is metal that is tucked into the mortar joints of a chimney above each piece of step flashing; it extends down and over the top of the step flashing to provide an effective watershed for the roof. The key advantage of counter flashing is that it allows the roof structure and chimney to move independently (in high winds or an earthquake) without separating from or damaging the roofing material attached to the base flashing and roof deck.

Just remember: all flashing around any vertical protrusion in the roof should be step and counter flashed. In addition, behind the chimney, where a sloping roofline meets the back (creating the most severe water and snow trap), many roofers also will install a cricket, or saddle. It looks like a miniature pitched roof, with a center ridge sloping up to the back side of the chimney or addition, creating two slopes that divert water from rain or melting snow around each side. If you've got a roof that slopes into a chimney, a cricket is essential and should not increase the cost of the overall roof job.

Your roofer also should install a drip edge at the eaves and rake edges to keep water from running down the roof and back up underneath the roofing material. Like other flashing, a continuous drip edge along the length of the eaves and rake edges is installed on the roof deck (or sheathing), then molded to a curvature that directs water to the gutter system or away from the house.

Finally, your roofer should take care to fasten the flashing and the finished roofing material with nails or screws that are of the same material as the flashing. Failure to do so will cause a chemical reaction between the two metals.

As there are many roof forms and a variety of roofing materials from which to choose — ranging in price, appearance, installation method and weight — if installed properly, any one of them can do the job. The question is, which one best suits your needs, budget and style of home?

Although I recommend reroofing with the same material originally used on the house, I realize doing so may present problems for many reasons. For most

Cedar shingles are installed in various degrees of overlap depending on the pitch of the roof. A 4-in-12 roof (one that rises 4 inches vertically for each horizontal foot typically requires a three-shingle buildup. Note that the shingles also overlap the edge of the structure, a feature that creates a drip edge for water.

reroofing jobs, the next best choice is asphalt composition shingles, or comp roofing. Comp roofing is the best combination of price and performance today, with manufacturer warranties running 20 years or more. It's also available in a multitude of appearances, including some that you'd swear from the curb are slate or wood shingles.

Now, if you're asking if I suggest substituting a modern product for the sake of convenience, I'm not — necessarily. First, not all building materials used 50 or 100 years ago were optimum for their purpose or climate; they were simply the best material available at the time. Also, a strict replacement of an historic roofing material such as slate may be cost-prohibitive today.

Second, and more important, asphalt composition roofing isn't modern by American building standards. In the mid-1800s, the first comp roofing — cloth or felt soaked in tar — was developed as a leakproof material for flat roofs, which were predominant in urban areas. Manufactured in large sheets, it presented fewer seams and voids, thus mitigating water infiltration. (This particular use is a great example of a material not exactly suited to its application; comp roofing on flat surfaces has since been replaced by better materials and methods.) However, comp shingles didn't become popular on the pitched roofs of single-family homes until the 1920s, during our country's first big housing boom, when they provided a low-cost, easy-to-install and durable alternative. Since then, comp roofing has improved dramatically in quality.

Last but not least, I subscribe to a preservation concept that says "Do No Harm," which is especially applicable to the roof. Using good-quality comp shingles doesn't change the structure or form of a roof and even can provide an adequate simulation of more traditional or historic roofing materials. Also, comp shingles don't preclude you from replacing them down the road with cedar shingles, slate, clay tiles or whatever was original to the home.

Asphalt composition shingles, like most roofing materials, are referred to by weight, as in 300-pound shingles. This number refers to the shingle's weight per square, in roofing terms, an area measuring 10x10 feet, or 100 square feet. A shingle's weight indicates its durability; the more it weighs, the longer it is expected to last. Some heavyweight comp shingles (weighing upwards of 380 pounds per square) carry warranties of 30 or 40 years, sometimes more. For most reroofing jobs, I recommend a minimum 240-pound, three-tab asphalt comp shingle. A three-tab profile is one in which the shingle panel is separated into three sections by slender notches, which serve to drain water away from the shingles; installation also is easier and therefore more cost-effective.

Since first being introduced, comp shingles have evolved dramatically in diversity of appearance. Manufacturers, ingeniously, have arranged various colors and sizes of the mineral-based granules on the felt–tar base to replicate shadows, wood and even stone. In addition, some of today's comp shingles feature a random or staggered edge on the exposed shingle (as opposed to edges that align, or are square-butted). Others can be laminated together to create a deeper profile on the roof. As these options enhance the aesthetics, they also typically boost the weight

Asphalt shingle installation begins with adequately underlaying roofing felt over sheathing, positioning the metal flashing in valleys (top) and around vent pipes and chimneys (not shown) and nailing each shingle to overlap in a pattern required by the pitch.

and cost, from a base price of about $30 per square for a 240-pound material to upwards of $95 per square for a heavyweight, designer shingle.

Unlike cedar shingles (discussed later in this chapter), asphalt shingles are installed over a solid roof deck of sheathing panels. While it's common to see $\frac{1}{2}$-inch oriented strand board (OSB) panels on such jobs, I still lean toward thicker, three-ply plywood, which should be nailed to the rafters and installed with metal clips at the seams to keep the panels flush (or flat) along the surface. Over the sheathing comes a layer of rolled-out felt paper, usually weighing 15 to 30 pounds (also indicating its weight per square), which acts as a watershed and moisture barrier to protect the wood below.

If your tear-off reveals spaced decking, I (and local codes, typically) recommend attaching new sheathing panels (plywood or OSB) over the existing deck. Few codes will allow you to fill the slots with comparably sized boards, and I'm wary of the practice because the new lumber never exactly matches the old decking boards and may react differently in freeze-thaw cycles. The result will be a wavy appearance on the roof's surface.

Assuming you select a three-tab asphalt shingle, either with a square-butt or random edge, the shingle tab slots (or rows) should align every other course, creating an effective drainage system and handsome appearance. Some roofers recommend alignment every three courses, but I think the aesthetic benefit of a more dimensional-looking roof is marginal, and the effectiveness of the notches as drainage channels may be reduced.

A finished reroof — whether with organic or inorganic asphalt shingle — provides a durable, waterproof shell that protects the house. The difference is in longevity: choose organic.

Organic vs. inorganic composition shingles

Organic and inorganic composition shingles are available in several different profiles, in laminated configurations and heavyweight versions. The difference in performance lies under the surface.

Organic shingles consist of a core, or base material, made of rag or cellulose fibers saturated with asphalt and coated with colored granules on one side. These granules are engineered to protect the base from UV rays and fire, and are designed to provide color and add dimension to the shingles. By its organic nature, however, this roofing material typically achieves only a Class C fire rating — the lowest — and comes with shorter warranties than its inorganic counterpart.

Inorganic shingles, by contrast, have a fiberglass mat, also covered with granules, which protects the surface; they typically achieve a Class A fire rating, meaning the material doesn't allow the spread of flames. (The transfer of sparks from one roof to another was blamed for the extensive damage caused by the 1991 Oakland hills fire in California. Some building codes require new and reroofed homes to have a Class A–rated roof, which is achieved most efficiently with fiberglass comp roofing.)

However, I've seen too many inorganic shingles buckle or delaminate within only a few years after installation, so I'm still uncomfortable recommending them over organic asphalt comp shingles.

Starting from the eaves, the shingles are attached to the sheathing with special roofing nails (called teco nails) or with what's called ring-shanks — nails with threads of raised rings along their length that help hold the fasteners to the deck for homes with steep roof pitches or those in high-wind areas. The nails should be driven carefully through the top portion of the shingles to the roof deck. If they are overdriven, this will expose the base of the shingle to water infiltration (and therefore premature deterioration), even though the fasteners will be covered by the exposed (or lower) portion of the next course of shingles. The same holds true for any and all roofing types (detailed further in this chapter). As for fastening shingles with staples, the staple crown (or top portion) invariably sets below the surface of the shingle, weakening it dramatically.

Finally, asphalt shingles are best installed in hot weather — not so hot that they soften to where working or walking on them causes tears or slipped granules but warm enough that the base material is fully expanded. If you must have the roof installed in cold weather, small gaps should be left between the shingles along each course to allow for expansion once the weather heats up; if not, even a fraction of an inch can spell trouble.

Next to asphalt comp shingles, the most popular and recommended roofing material is cedar. About a hundred years ago, cedar shingles were the predominant roofing material for American homes, and no wonder: they were easy to install and plentiful in major population areas, making them relatively inexpensive, as well.

The same is true today, where cedar shingles commonly are found still on homes along the timber baskets of the North, Intermountain West and Pacific Northwest, as well as on historic preservation and restoration projects nationwide.

Cedar shingle roofs take advantage of the wood's natural decay- and climate-resistant qualities. Milled and crafted from a tree's heartwood, the shingles are made from the long, narrow grain of the wood's fiber to maintain their shape and effectiveness over a long period of time.

Today, most wood shingles are available in white or red cedar. Like most solid wood products, both varieties are offered in grades of lumber; the lower the grade, the lower the quality and durability of the shingles. The only grade you need to remember for red cedar is #1 perfection or blue label, either of which is comparable in quality to those hand-sawn shingles of the past. In fact, modern machine-sawn-and-tapered cedar shingles don't differ all that much in their appearance or performance from those shaped with a draw knife back in the 1890s. Properly installed and maintained, a cedar shingle roof will last 50 years or more, just like they did a century ago.

If your home's original roof was cedar shingles, tear-off likely will reveal the spaced sheathing mentioned before. Unlike reroofing with asphalt comp shingles, you don't have to put down solid sheathing. The spaced decking (with any necessary repairs, of course) will serve as a ventilation system. In fact, without it, cedar shingles would suffocate.

This thin shake roof needed minor repair, so several split or deteriorated cedar shingles were replaced. The new shakes will soon weather in, blending with the color of the older shingles. While this maintenance will add a few more years to the life of the roof, eventually the patching will be inadequate and a complete new roof will be required.

The Shake Myth Let's quickly correct a case of mistaken history. During the last 20 years or so, I've seen several folks install cedar shakes, the untapered, thicker brethren of cedar shingles, in an apparent attempt to be more authentic. But using shakes is a sure sign you haven't done your homework. Few craftsmen of the early twentieth century would have used shakes to roof a house. Shakes were typically relegated to a barn or shed, where appearances and performance were less critical. (Besides, shakes are a pain to put on; their thickness requires longer, thicker nails, which often split the layers of material over the roof decking, creating the potential for leaks.)

Spaced decking allows a cedar-shingled roof to dry out after a snow- or rainstorm, helping to maintain the shingles' shape and therefore their effectiveness. If you see a contemporary house with cedar shingles that appear ragged, broken, warped or upturned, it's often a sign that they were installed over a solid roof deck. The result? The effective life of the material is reduced by 15 to 20 years, less than half what it would be with proper installation and maintenance.

If there is a compelling reason to reroof with cedar shingles over solid sheathing (for instance, if you're tearing off an old comp roof with a solid deck, or your attic has been finished as living space), I've found a new product that allows proper ventilation between the sheathing and the new wood shingles. Cedar Breather, from Benjamin-Obdyke in Warminster, Pennsylvania [(800) 346-7655], is a $\frac{3}{8}$-inch-thick nylon mesh that attaches on top of the sheathing. Like felt for an asphalt comp roof, Cedar Breather comes in long rolls, so its easy to install over the roof decking; the shingles are then nailed through the mesh to the sheathing. Used with a continuous ridge vent (which circulates stuffy air out of the attic along the roof's peak), this product will ventilate cedar shingles effectively.

Installing cedar shingles, like asphalt comp shingles, is a relatively fast process; sure, there are more shingles to nail down compared to a three-tab comp, but an experienced, professional roofer can work almost mechanically, yet with an old-world, craftsman style. It's actually fun to watch.

Your roof's pitch will determine how much of each cedar shingle will be exposed; the lower the pitch, the less exposure you want because water doesn't shed as

quickly off a shallower slope. As a general rule, you should see only about a third of the butt-end of a shingle exposed, meaning there are three layers of material between the exposed roof and the sheathing, providing a tight seal. Shingles on the first (or starter) course should be doubled to achieve this layering from the eaves to the ridge.

Unlike asphalt shingles, which are manufactured with gaps between the tabs, cedar shingles are single units, so your roofer should leave narrow gaps between them to allow for expansion and contraction in various climate conditions (if they're held too tight to one another they'll buckle). However, the gaps should not align vertically from course to course because this will create a severe water channel.

Given the random widths of cedar shingles (as opposed to the uniform size of asphalt shingles), the outer edges should be at least $1\frac{1}{2}$ inches away from any gaps left by junctions between shingles on the course below, again to prevent excessive water from running between the shingles. And no shingle wider than 8 or 10 inches should be installed whole; if it isn't split now, it surely will split on its own later. Last, the shingles should overhang the eaves by about 2 inches and by an inch so on the side edges of the roof, or include a drip edge to direct water runoff to the gutters and away from the sidewalls.

While asphalt comp and cedar shingles have dominated American roofs for the better part of this century, architectural styles and regional resources have created demand for and use of other roofing materials. Clay, stone and metal, each available in various types, sizes, styles and colors, have specific design and functional characteristics.

It usually takes three full rows of asphalt shingles to cover a single point on the roof, each overlapping the others by one-third to ensure proper water drainage (top). A shingle roof doesn't have asphalt's advantage in this regard: wood shingles along each course are positioned to catch water from the row above, and should run in staggered rows at least $1\frac{1}{2}$ inches apart.

For geographic and cultural reasons, clay and ceramic tile most often is seen on roofs in the Gulf and Desert states. What most people don't know is that ceramic tiles, such as those mission-style half-rounds you see in Arizona and Florida, were used on homes dating back to Colonial days. Lighter and less expensive than their slate counterparts at the time, ceramic and clay tile provided a tougher, longer-lasting shell than wood for these climates.

When using any cementitious or stone material, the structure underneath it — in this case the roof rafters — must be engineered to handle the extra weight of the tiles. Also, the fasteners must not be overdriven and should be at least 2 inches away from the rake edges and eaves; failure in both cases has been blamed for the extensive damage caused by flying roof tiles during Hurricane Andrew in South Florida a few years back.

Slate roofing also has its roots in early American housing. The fire-resistant qualities of slate far outstripped those of thatch and other traditional European materials; moreover, it was plentiful from the quarries of the northeastern United States. A tour of Colonial-style homes in areas such as Virginia and Pennsylvania reveal the wide variety of slate roof designs and patterns used then and simulated now (usually with specially designed asphalt composition shingles or lightweight concrete compositions) for their ornamental and functional qualities.

1 A ceramic tile roof is distinctive and decorative, giving no question about the style of the house.

2 Rubberoid fabric roofing, available in sheets and rolls, is manufactured to simulate an asphalt shingle roof but requires no layering. Because of this, the weight of the roof is reduced — but so is its ability to protect the dwelling. It usually is seen on low-pitch or flat roofs.

3 Sheet metal roofing is durable and water-resistant in all climates. It is available in galvanized (zinc-dipped) steel, aluminum and copper.

4 We usually think of cedar shingles as only along the plane of a roof, but it also can be formed around curves and bevels to create a designer
finish equal in aesthetics to the thatch roofs found on some English-style cottages.

5 Natural slate roofs, while traditional features of many older homes, are extremely heavy compared to modern wood shingles and their alternatives. They require strong support bracing, rafters and joists.

Today, the use of true slate roofing is hindered by availability, price and weight; like concrete and ceramic tile, a slate roof can weigh upwards of 700 pounds per square, almost three times that of standard asphalt shingles. If your roof structure is designed to support them, today's slate roofing tiles feature predrilled shingles to make installation faster and easier, and they come in a wide variety of colors and patterns to maintain historical designs.

If you want to understand the value of a metal roof, there's a now-classic photo from the fire in the Oakland hills area of northern California in 1991 showing a single, metal-roofed house standing amid the rubble of its neighbors. Sparks flying from the wind-driven fires on cedar shingle roofs died out on the non-combustible metal; not surprisingly, during rebuilding in the area, several people opted for metal roofing to protect their homes from the next firestorm.

Along with its fire resistance, there are several other advantages to metal roofing. It is lightweight, perhaps half or even less that of a recommended-weight asphalt comp roof. It reflects radiant heat away from the house, minimizing heat build-up in the attic. Because it typically is installed in continuous sheets (or panels) from the ridge to the eaves, it can be used on low-slope (3-in-12) roofs and still effectively shed water and snow runoff. Finally, metal roofs are now available in several patterns, colors, textures and styles, including some that even simulate half-round, mission-style ceramic tiles through layering and colored stone granules.

The downside? The price of the material and its installation, which can run twice that of asphalt comp roofing. But a properly installed and maintained metal roof can last a century or more, thus lowering life-cycle costs to well below the expense of reroofing with asphalt at least three times during that time span. Another potential downside is the noise, such as during a rain- or hailstorm. Some folks like it; those who don't should consider metal roof systems with integral foam insulation to deaden the clatter.

Metal roofing, in the form of terne (tin- or lead-coated iron), was first popularized in the late 1800s, but as is the case today with terne flashing, the material must be regularly painted to maintain its performance. Today, metal roofing is available mainly in three basic materials: copper, aluminum and coated steel. Copper is the most desired but most expensive, about double the cost of other metal roofing alternatives. Easily worked and requiring no applied coatings for protection, it weathers to a reddish brown and, later, to its renown pale green hue.

Like copper, aluminum resists corrosion and doesn't require a coating for protection; it's also the least expensive of the materials, running about $3 a square foot installed for panels, less for aluminum shingles. In fact, a mill-finish (or uncoated) aluminum roof develops a colorless oxide layer, which is somewhat water soluble, meaning it will repair minor scrapes and scratches on its own by oxidizing the damage over time. Painted aluminum roofing offers even more protection but must be periodically maintained.

Steel roofing almost always is coated, typically with a galvanized (or zinc-based) layer. This coating provides what's called a sacrificial layer, which corrodes over time for the sake of maintaining the quality of the steel underneath; it also

Though expensive when compared to other metal roofing materials, copper is extremely durable and easy to install. The distinctive standing seams of metal roofs are joined by cross-folded tabs or rivets, soldered, then covered with a V-shaped flashing to complete each seam. No nails are used on the weather surface.

means it must be painted after a few years to prevent rusting. Aluminum, as opposed to zinc, offers a more permanent coating for a steel roof; you also may find coatings that are formulated to repel dirt and UV light. Steel roofing typically runs slightly higher than aluminum, up to about $4 a square foot installed.

As mentioned above, metal differs from other roofing materials in its installation. Most metal roofs are applied as 2-foot-wide panels (called "pans") that run continuously from ridge to eaves. These panels interlock with one another, creating a watertight seam that reduces the number of joints and conceals the fasteners that hold the roof to the deck.

To balance quality control and speed of installation, some metal-roofing contractors have invested in pan fabrication equipment that creates the panels and seams on the job site, but it is a more expensive proposition. Several suppliers offer factory-made, preformed pans in a variety of dimensions, colors and styles. But beware: metal roofing off the rack may be clipped together at the joints instead of seamed, requiring careful flashing and fastener protection. In addition, because metal reacts to climate changes more dramatically than many other roofing materials, clips, gaskets and other connectors on factory-supplied metal roofs may loosen over time.

A few other tips: If you live in snow country, ask your roofer about snow jacks, which are slight projections that help snow grip the slick metal instead of cascading off the eaves. Also, as we discussed with flashing, make sure all metal pieces are of the same type, including gutters and downspouts, to prevent corrosion and staining. Wet mortar from a new or restored chimney also can react with metal roofing, so paint or coat directly adjacent areas.

Finally, a word about flat roofs, which really aren't flat at all but instead have a slight, nearly undetectable slope (perhaps $\frac{1}{4}$ inch per foot) to facilitate water runoff to the gutters or other drainage systems. Still, that's flat enough to allow water to pool after a heavy rain- or snowstorm, requiring that you select and seal a material that can hold standing water for hours or even days and take the heat of the sun and UV rays without drying up or cracking. Initially, with the growth of urban areas, rolls of composition roofing were used to cover the usually flat surfaces of commercial and residential buildings. But newer technology now almost exclusively dictates use of rubberized and plastic materials for these roof applications.

The most popular is rubberized EPDM (for Ethylene Propylene Diene Monomer). EPDM requires no fasteners, flashing or caulking; rather, it is installed over the entire surface of the roof, often in one piece, with a cove (or curved mold) at its connection with the sidewalls to direct water away from the corners and edges. The material itself is watertight (and also may be installed under a sloped roof material, such as comp shingles, to provide even more protection for the roof sheathing and attic).

I've received a few questions over the years about PVC for flat roofs, but as far as I'm concerned, the jury's still out on its effectiveness. Its main hitch: PVC tends to shrink when it gets warm (the opposite of other roofing materials), which can

Seasonal debris — usually leaves and twigs but sometimes moss growing in muddy deposits — will quickly clog downspouts and cause gutters to overflow. Maintenance once every season is the answer.

allow water infiltration. Newer versions claim to be improved, but I'm skeptical, especially when I hear PVC offered at a lower price than EPDM, a much more time-tested product. In short, I think you'll get what you pay for.

Before we climb off the roof and move down the walls, let's not forget the gutters, downspouts and other systems for properly channeling and carrying water away from the house (we'll see the effects of not having them when we to discuss foundation problems later in this chapter). While there are historic considerations to ponder, it is much more critical to have a system that does the job effectively with simple, regular maintenance.

Gutters, which usually follow the eaves of the roof, are the main carriers of runoff to strategically placed downspouts. Besides simply failing to clean them out twice a year, I see people make two main mistakes with their gutters: installing the length of gutter to an incorrect pitch or slope to the downspouts and improperly strapping the gutters to the fascia (or front portion of the roof structure, at or under the eaves).

Like flat roofs, gutters are slightly pitched to direct water. It's really a balancing act; you want the gutters to slope toward the downspouts but not so much that it makes the roof look out of line. A good rule is about $1/_{16}$ inch per foot. Over long stretches, where such a slope would cause the gutter to run off the bottom of the fascia at one end, the typical solution is to slope it from the middle to two downspouts on the ends or to break the run somewhere in the middle with a single downspout.

Most premanufactured gutters arrive with fastening and strapping components. Take heed of the directions, especially where two sections of 8- or 10-foot gutters join, then make sure to inspect them and the joint seals after heavy rains and during your fall and spring whole-house maintenance regimen. For those too forgetful (or maybe just repelled) to clean the gunk out of the gutters, consider attaching welded, galvanized metal screening over the tops to keep leaves, twigs and other debris out but still allow water in.

As important as how your gutters are installed is their size. Most homes have 5-inch gutters, which often are inadequate to handle a heavy rain or runoff from snow. In most cases, 6-inch gutters will do the job. Better still, ask your roofer to select the proper size gutters for the weather in your area and point out the spots on the roof that will drain the most runoff.

Once the water gets to the downspouts, it is important to make sure they're free of debris and also can carry the water at least 6 feet away from the base of the wall, preferably to a splash block that further disperses the water before it touches the ground or to an underground drainage system. I recommend a 4-inch downspout (as opposed to the typical 3-inch), to get the water out of the gutter more quickly.

Depending on your home's architectural style, you'll want to install gutters that meet your historic and functional needs. The most common gutter is the K-style, a seamless, continuous length of aluminum formed (or molded) on the job site with integral grooves and ledges to secure connections. A more historically correct

"The drip edges and gutter system of

your roof plays a critical role in

weatherproofing your house. Keep it

clean of seasonal debris and in

good repair at all times."

– BOB YAPP

and architecturally appropriate style is the half-round. More sleek and therefore less obtrusive than the K-style, half-rounds are more difficult to strap and fasten to the fascia, however. (In my travels, I've come across Commercial Gutter Systems of Kalamazoo, Michigan, which makes rigid, stainless steel and copper-coated stainless steel roof rods that eliminate strapping problems.) Half-rounds also may be more difficult to come by in your area, which may boost their cost and reduce your selection of sizes and colors.

Finally, like the ones installed on homes a century ago, you may want to opt for built-in gutters, which are framed as part of the eaves and soffit assembly, the underside of the rafters that extends beyond the roof. Because these gutters are made of wood, they require extra protection. In the past, it was a copper lining; today, it is most likely an EPDM lining, by far the cheaper — if less historical — alternative. But then, if you're considering a custom, built-in gutter system, perhaps cost isn't your biggest concern.

Siding　When people set out simply to remodel rather than restore and preserve an older home, they're apt to make exterior and interior changes more according to their personal tastes. But I believe, deep down, something about the home's original character attracted them in the first place and that stripping the house of its historic qualities only will sacrifice that initial infatuation.

Nowhere else is this displayed more tragically than on the facades and exterior details of older homes. From covering up classic wood clapboard siding with vinyl to bricking in a doorway or enclosing a wraparound porch, the damage to a home's character, history, value and performance can be devastating.

Proper restoration and preservation of a home's exterior has as much to do with using original materials and textures as it does with replicating the techniques that achieved them. Such texturing is especially significant on masonry walls of brick or stucco, where the brick course design, mortar joints and trowel patterns are subtle, yet key, trademarks of the home.

Restoring the exterior of your home also affords the opportunity to uncover and fix behind-the-wall problems that can undermine the long-term performance of the home's exterior and interior finishes.

All the behind-the-wall repairs in the world, however, won't mitigate by far the most damaging thing you can do to the sidewalls of your old house, which is to cover its original wood or masonry exterior with replacement vinyl or aluminum siding. Not only do these materials have no place on an historic facade, they are made from nonrenewable resources like petroleum and ore.

If you think it costs less to install replacement siding rather than restore and maintain a home's original exterior, think again: over a 20-year period, the cost to hire a carpenter and contract for two high-quality paint jobs is less than putting on vinyl siding and having to replace or paint it when it deteriorates. More important, in neighborhoods undergoing renovation, appraisers invariably will dock a home with replacement siding, lowering its value.

This gingerbread-trimmed beauty seems to be wearing a tiara, proclaiming its right to be respected when exterior repairs are necessary. Hopefully, the owners will continue their careful maintenance of the structure in tribute to days long gone when the evidence of such craftsmanship was the norm, not the exception.

But worse than any impact on maintenance costs or resale value is that replacement siding products, installed over original siding, can damage the structure of your house without you even knowing it — until it's too late. Unlike wood or masonry siding, they create a barrier against moisture generated by cooking and bathing that looks to escape from the inside of your house. Combined with insulation blown into the sidewalls (another favorite remodeling job, discussed in Chapter Three), this outside vapor barrier traps moisture and holds it in the wall cavity.

The result is an accumulation of moisture that will condensate and, over time, collect at the sill plate, which rests on the foundation and holds the vertical stud walls. Ultimately, this will render your insulation ineffective and create a haven for termites and other pests. The combination of rot and infestation can lead to significant, if not irreversible, structural damage.

Once you discover what replacement siding can do to your walls, you'll agree that terms like "permanent" and "maintenance-free" associated with vinyl and aluminum siding are, at best, misnomers. (At worst, they're false advertising.)

Vinyl siding warps and fades over a period of five to ten years, especially on the west-facing side, where the sun and its ultraviolet rays are strongest. Such fading, while subtle, means you never can replace a piece of damaged, warped or missing vinyl siding with

Disappearing Beauty

The beautiful details of this home are about to be covered up, and it likely will lose its structural integrity over time. Owners are frequently under the mistaken belief that nonwood siding will eliminate the need for painting and maintenance. How sad!

Gone forever The beautiful architectural details of this finely crafted heritage home are quickly disappearing beneath an ill-advised application of vinyl siding.

The decision not to restore the home will probably be irreversible because of the shoddy construction habits shown. The original siding and moldings are being covered by a new, nonbreathing layer of vinyl, meaning all moisture inside the house will be trapped.

Within a few years, the condensed moisture likely will begin to rot the original siding and its supporting framing. Before too long, the whole house will become structurally unsound.

Once vinyl or aluminum siding is installed, the decay process cannot be stopped without a wholesale removal of it and the underlying structure.

Such siding installations, when they *are* appropriate, always require great care to insulate and ventilate the underlying structure. Continuous vents must be installed at the junctions of the wall with the foundation and roof, to permit good air flow from bottom to top. A vapor barrier must be installed on the inside of every outside wall.

a true match. Furthermore, it is very difficult to get a quality, long-lasting paint job on faded vinyl siding. The material is not formulated to hold most paints, and it may shrink and/or soften depending on the color and formulation of the paint.

As for aluminum siding, it will eventually chalk after about 20 years; that is, its finish and coating will deteriorate to a fine powder you can rub off with your hand. Then, it must be thoroughly cleaned, primed, painted and maintained. And, oh yes, aluminum siding is susceptible to dents and scratches from hail, tree branches and kids' bikes, which also means the material will have to be replaced and maintained. Permanent? Maintenance-free? Hardly.

By far a better alternative to replacement siding in terms of investment, historical value, aesthetics and even long-term maintenance is to preserve and restore the home's original exterior, whether cedar, redwood or masonry.

For homes with wood siding, that means paint, which also means a thorough, high-quality preparation of the structure and the surface. Proper preparation starts with a complete inspection of the original siding and detailing. If you discover or uncover moisture damage, usually revealed by peeling or blistering paint, the first task is to find the source of the moisture and eliminate it. Solving chronic moisture problems (or pest infestation) will give your restored siding a chance to live a full life with minimal maintenance.

Next, remove and replace all damaged sections with the same type of wood, making sure your new siding has a moisture content of no more than 13 percent; much more and the wood will shrink as its dries, causing problems with the

The only thing certain about aluminum siding is its eminent destruction of distinctive architectural trim work and moldings.

About hardboard and other wood-based siding

For the last 30 years or so, economic and environmental concerns have driven the development and use of engineered wood siding — panels that resemble wood but are made from compressed wood fibers or paper, adhesives, wax and other binders. Such hardboard products weigh more than solid wood siding but are installed and painted similarly to their counterparts. They may even come pre-painted or with a molded wood grain on the exposed face.

Early on, these products were not manufactured to the highest performance standards, especially when it came to factory-applied primers and the paraffin wax used in the product's composition. Moisture penetrated the weak primer, and the wax was known to bleed through to the surface, causing discoloration. Repainting them required complete coverage with a high-quality primer and sealing all joints and vulnerable areas before painting the surface.

More recent versions of hardboard siding have addressed these concerns, but they still have their problems. In warm, moist climates, like the Gulf states, such siding has experienced swelling. Like a sponge, the siding soaks up moisture, either from a poor factory finish or from vapor generated from the inside of the house condensing on the unfinished back side of the panels.

At best, a hardboard siding job will last 15 years before it needs to be repaired, sections replaced and repainted. A better, longer-lasting bet: Cedar lap siding.

fasteners, joint connections and the replacement piece itself. Also, set aside all details, such as shutters, storm windows and trim, to prep and restore before you reinstall them on the house.

You'll also want to research past paint jobs (unless you plan to take the current exterior finish down to the bare wood) to make sure the new layer will adhere to the older paints. For instance, it's okay to paint latex over oil-based paints or primers but not the other way around.

First, take off as much of the old paint as possible, although there are definitely correct and incorrect ways to go about it. High-pressure washing or sandblasting are unacceptable because they damage the wood and render a surface that won't accept and hold primer and paint. The same is true for sanding and grinding or any method that gets below the surface of the wood. Scraping is an acceptable option, but it must be done very carefully or it can gouge the surface. I've found that a handheld, carbide-blade scraper will remove loose paint effectively and leave a clean surface for new primer and paint coatings.

If you dread hours of hand scraping, I recommend the Paint Shaver by American-International Tool Company. This electric hand tool removes paint from all exposed surfaces of the siding, as well as the underside of the butt edges along each course. Its three

1 Exterior painting begins with the thorough removal of all old, flaking and peeling paint, usually through mechanical stripping with a scraper or electric paint shaver.

2 Masking windows and their frames will save much cleanup work later in the painting project. At the same time, frames should be resealed where they join the siding with permanent waterproof caulk, and any holes or spits should be puttied.

3 A big mistake — using a power washer on siding. Power washing causes water to penetrate every crack and surface defect, making a good sealing job impossible. I never recommend it.

4 Repairs should precede the painting. Here, a siding panel has been opened to replace wood that has developed dry rot from leaks around the window casing.

5 The finished product is a beautifully painted home that has had all of its surface defects repaired and joints sealed, making it waterproof. This paint job shouldn't require renewal for more than a decade.

triangle-shaped blades, which can be adjusted to minimize the removal of bare wood, turn paint into dust, which then can be collected into a hepa vacuum (like a shop vac) through a dust shroud to keep it from escaping.

Once you're down to the base wood, have repaired the source of any moisture infiltration from the roof or inside the wall cavity and replaced missing or damaged sections, your siding is ready to clean. I recommend a solution of $\frac{1}{2}$ cup TSP mixed with a gallon of water, then rinsing with a hose and allowing it to air dry. This will remove any dust, grime, loose paint chips and other debris that will hinder the primer and paint's ability to adhere to the wood. Avoid harsh chemical cleaners and solutions, which may damage or remove valuable textures, colors or pigments. Once the surface has been cleaned and is dry, the most vulnerable spots, such as joints where water could seep in as it cascades down the sidewalls, should be gone over with a siliconized latex caulk. Such sealants are formulated to expand and contract with climate changes (thereby maintaining their seal) and can be primed and painted. I try to get homeowners to think of their house as sitting under a waterfall — the only areas that need caulking are those where water coming down the sidewalls can get in.

This kind of thorough preparation will ensure that the paint will go on smoothly and adhere to the wood, meaning the job also will last much longer. As a result, your maintenance chores are reduced to seasonal touch-ups, with repainting perhaps every 10 to 15 years if you remove all the previous paint, about 7 to 9 years if you leave patches of previous paint jobs on the surface.

With the prep work done, it's time to prime the bare wood for the finish coat of paint. Assuming you're working with aged wood (as opposed to new wood), the best primer is alkyd oil-based; it soaks into the wood better, promoting preservation of the fibers, which, in turn, reduces peeling on the surface.

Sure, painting your house (including all the prep work) can be a daunting task if you decide to do the job yourself. But here's a trick to keep your enthusiasm high: after you inspect, repair and replace the siding, tackle only one side of the house at a time, from scraping and cleaning to the final coat of paint. Completing one side at a time will show daily progress, keep your sanity and not require you to rush through a stage if there's bad weather on the horizon.

Finally, if you're considering a darker paint color, consider applying a tinted primer, which may allow you to get by with one coat of paint. Remember, a gallon of paint typically covers about 350 square feet of wall surface with one coat. Check your math to determine the right amount to buy. That said, add a gallon of primer and a few extra gallons of paint and store them in a dry area at room temperature. You'll thank me later.

If time isn't a luxury you enjoy, an option I've come to rely on is factory-finished cedar clapboard siding. Primed and painted on all sides (including board ends and those that won't be exposed) and shipped with a quart or so of touch-up paint and nails colored to match the finish, it costs about 10 cents less per square foot to install than vinyl siding. Many are warranted for 15 years — up to 30 years if you specify two coats of paint.

Whatever kind of exterior your home has, proper and periodic maintenance will keep it looking great, typically without wholesale repainting for a dozen years or more. I usually do exterior home maintenance in the fall, to prepare for winter weather. I start by walking around my home and inspecting the condition of the sidewalls. I remove and replace worn or cracked caulking, and scrape and feather (or lightly sand) any peeling or chipped paint down to the bare wood. Now, here's where that inventory of primer and paint pay off, because they will match the color of the paint job.

Foundations We're now at the base of your old house, the foundation upon which the structure and everything attached to it rests. Though its functional value is obvious, I bet you don't think of it as an area with any aesthetics or character. Not so.

Many homes older than 50 years have a brick or stone foundation that is exposed above grade (or ground level), creating a distinctive skirt that even may extend to porch columns or other exterior accents. If so, your foundation is an important part of your home's overall character and should be restored and maintained with as much consideration for its appearance as for its performance.

As with your roofing and siding, your foundation is most under attack from moisture infiltration. A structural engineer I know is fond of saying that the only way to guarantee a dry basement is to build on a slab foundation. But if you have an older home built over a crawl space or a basement, you have little choice but to tend to your foundation with periodic maintenance and repair.

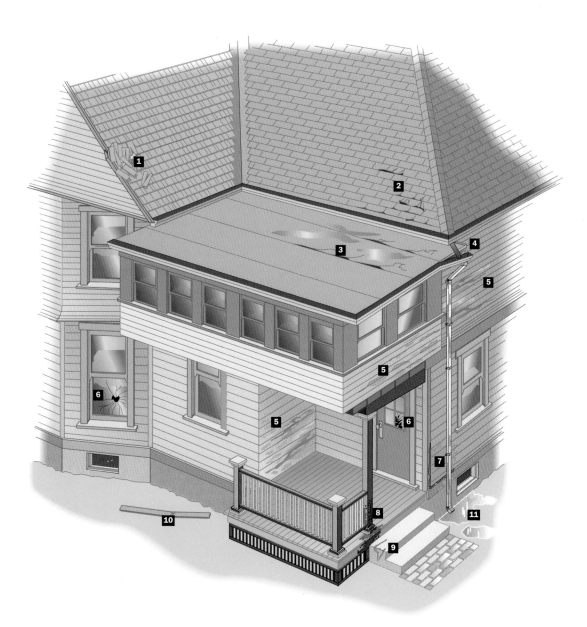

Exterior Maintenance

1 Cracked and damaged cedar shingles

2 Worn, curled and broken comp shingles

3 Worn and leaking roofing material, inadequate slope

4 Broken downspout and leaking gutter

5 Cracked, peeling and mildewed paint

6 Broken glass and glazing

7 Dry rot and water damage

8 Termite insect infestation

9 Cracked concrete steps

10 Fallen drip edge molding

11 Missing slope, splash block and runout

Telltale signs of moisture damage include staining from efflorescence (the leaching of salts through the masonry and mortar), missing or worn mortar, surface damage or deformation, cracks and fissures. Whatever the problem, you'll want to find its source. The most likely places to look are water runoff from the roof and gutter system, paved areas around the house and drainage away from the foundation and its openings. If you've allowed your gutter system to fall into disrepair, or if it is too small to handle the runoff, it likely is allowing rain and melted snow to fall directly to the base of the house and infiltrate the foundation wall. Worse yet is a lack of extenders and splash blocks, which may be allowing water to drain right next to the house. If paved areas such as walkways and patios near or adjacent to the foundation aren't sloped to drain water away from the house, they also can become spillways into the foundation (not to mention the basement or crawl space).

Over time, water buildup will settle the backfill around your foundation (which should slope away at least 3 degrees to drain water effectively), and it may create voids in the soil that will allow the foundation to settle, or drop. Furthermore, the pressure created by the water against the foundation may cause the walls to bow and mortar to deteriorate between the bricks, compromising your home's structural integrity and precluding an extensive foundation overhaul.

If water runoff appears to be your culprit, the fixes are likely straightforward. First, repair the gutter system and install extenders and splash blocks. If paved areas slope to the house, replace them or jack them up. If water is getting into

Brick
and stucco may seem like
tougher, more durable siding
materials than wood, but they
can be as easily damaged
during restoration. When
bricks are fired in a kiln, the
exterior surfaces come out
much harder than the interior;
break one in half and you'll
see what I mean. As with
wood siding, abrasive treatments, such as sandblasting
and high-pressure water
blasting, can remove valuable
protective layers and expose
masonry to moisture infiltration.
Chances are, the surfaces
merely need to be cleaned or
the mortar joints repointed
(refilled) to restore them to
their original effectiveness. To
replace damaged or missing
bricks, find a salvage yard
that carries bricks as close to
the same period of your house
as possible. Aside from the
aesthetic inconsistency of
using them, new bricks are
made in larger and more

uniform dimensions and
generally are harder than the
older masonry, making them
near impossible to match with
an historic brick job.

With worn or damaged stucco,
you want to remove worn sections to the framing, exposing
each of the stucco's three
layers [see Chapter Three]
before attempting to apply any
new material. Restored sections
of stucco must follow the
original texture of the finish
coat, whether sweeping trowel
marks, stipple or smooth. I like
to see stucco left exposed to
weather naturally, but because
almost all stucco homes are
painted, I recommend you
invest in a high-quality paint
job to match the rest of the
exterior's color.

Painting brick, however, is a
different story. Those who
recommend painting over a
brick-sided house do so ration-
alizing that the paint will seal
the masonry units and mortar
from moisture. And it does,

but it also creates chronic
moisture and maintenance
problems by not allowing it to
ventilate properly.

To prepare brick for repair, take
care not to chip or remove any
of the surface. You'll also want
to repoint (or fill) any missing
mortar joints, making sure you
match the texture, indentation,
color and width of the original.
It also is important to repoint
with a mortar compound that
closely matches the original,
though it costs about $100
for a lab analysis.

Why go to such extremes?
Simply, brick and stone contract
and expand with changing
climate conditions, and bricks
may enlarge slightly over their
life span. Therefore, the mortar must not be harder than
the masonry or it will com-
press the bricks or stones and
cause cracks or flaking of the
surface. Mortar in older brick
homes was high in lime content, so come as close to
matching it as you can.

the basement through windows, find the source and fix it. Finally, for added protection, consider installing a window dam or clear plastic bubble over the opening; both solutions will block water but not light.

If you inspect and test your runoff systems and find them in good working order, water damage to your foundation may be from groundwater, either a high water table or poor drainage of water from a rain- or snowfall. Or, the culprit could be one of your trees or shrubs. Their roots attract moisture and hold it; perhaps one is pressing on the foundation wall below grade or seeking a crack to infiltrate. It may be disheartening to remove an old tree, but you could be saving yourself headaches and potentially devastating structural damage.

If it is clear you have a drainage problem that can't be alleviated by any of the previous measures, there are three basic ways to fix it. The first is what pros call a Beaver Dam® system, a perforated plastic drain installed around the perimeter of your basement or crawl space walls at the baseboard or wall-floor joint. Water is channeled through this system to a sump pit and pumped out.

Another solution is the French tile system, also installed along the interior of the foundation wall. With this system, a small, perimeter channel is cut out of the concrete floor along the wall; to collect water from the channel, a trench is dug next to the footing and filled a few inches with river rock. A perforated plastic pipe connected to a sump pump sits on top and is held in place with more rock. The trench is backfilled with dirt and patched on the surface to conceal it.

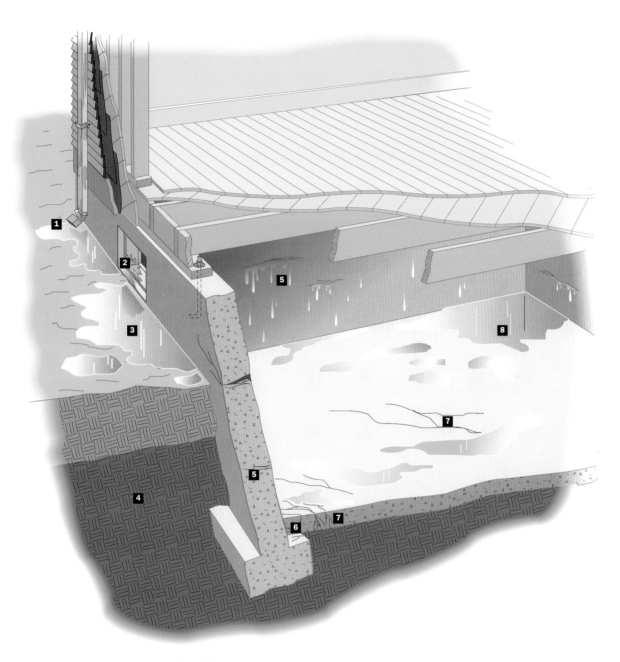

Leaking Basement

1. Inadequate runout for downspout
2. Window glazing failure
3. Inadequate-grade slope with standing water
4. High groundwater table
5. Masonry cracks, leaks and efflorescence
6. Weeping perimeter joint at foundation and floor edge
7. Cracked floor slab
8. Standing water

The third method is to dig a trench around the exterior of the foundation and install a perimeter drainage and foundation waterproofing system. A trench as deep as the footings is dug to slope away from the house toward a collection area covered with plastic that (like flashing on a chimney) runs up the foundation wall. A 2-inch bed of gravel is added to the trench; on top of that is laid a perforated or slotted pipe, typically of hard plastic (PVC) and measuring 3 to 4 inches in diameter. The pipe is laid around the foundation to meet at a single low point, where a solid section of at least 4 feet is extended away from the house to drain at grade. (This system, like the others, can also channel water to a sump pit in the basement, where it can be pumped out.)

The pipe in the trench is then covered with gravel (which helps filter the water of dirt and other debris). A weed control or other type of fiber mat is then laid on top of the gravel to prevent dirt from getting into the pipe. Finally, the dirt is added back into the trench and sloped 3 to 5 degrees away from the foundation wall. Now that oughta do it!

Now that you've solved the problem, the next step is to repair the damage. Going in, be aware that not every small crack needs to be patched. Rather, it's the large or expanding cracks, especially in key structural areas such as at corners, that are your main concern.

With brick and stone foundations, exposed and worn mortar joints will need to be repointed, that is, refilled with mortar to match the original application. Be sure the joints are tooled first to remove moisture and excess mortar. This process

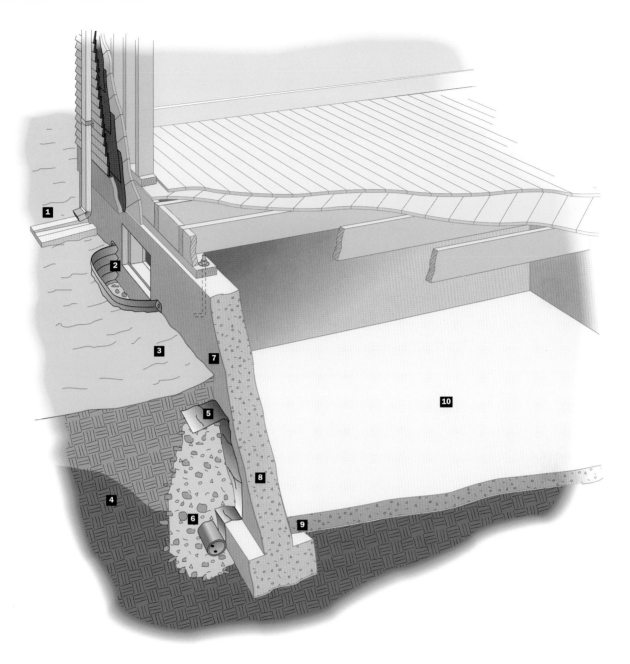

Dry Basement

1 Runout and splash block for downspout

2 Basement window dam

3 Grade sloping away from foundation

4 Groundwater table

5 Waterproof membrane

6 Perimeter drain of gravel and perforated plastic drainage pipe

7 Flexible polymer sealant

8 Caulked masonry cracks

9 Perimeter joint caulking

10 Sealed floor cracks

will restore the original appearance and create a waterproof seal. With older homes, however, today's high-quality mortar actually may cause damage to the softer brick, squeezing it until it crumbles or flakes. Ask your contractor or a masonry supplier to suggest a softer mortar.

If you have to replace a brick or section of masonry, do your best to find units that are about the same vintage instead of using new ones. Not only will there be a marked color and texture difference between the old and the new (thereby affecting the historical value of the house), but the new, harder bricks eventually will crush the older ones around them. Finally, be sure that the affected area is properly supported (or shored up) to carry the load of the structure above it as the repairs are made.

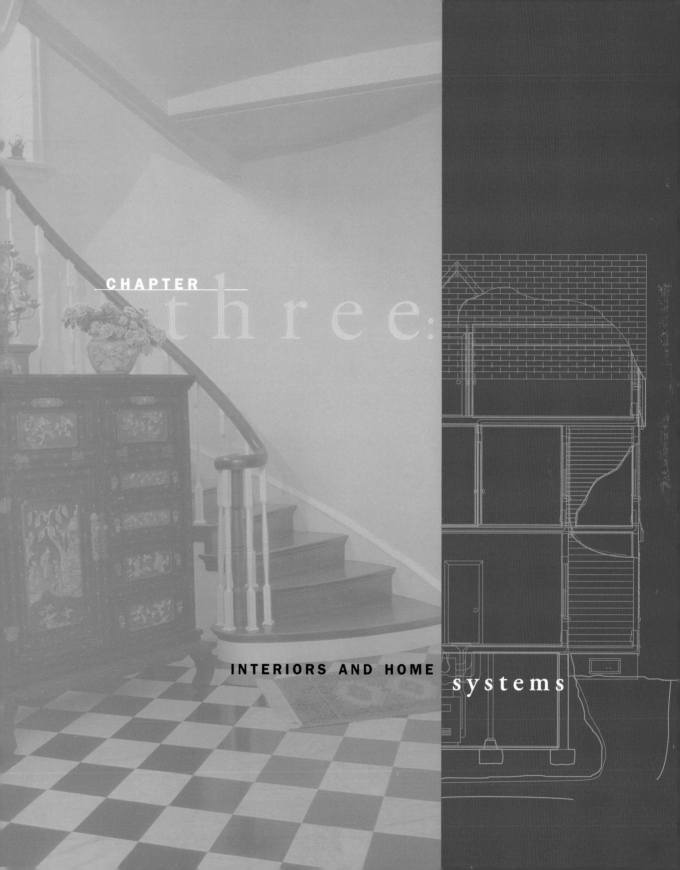

three:

INTERIORS AND HOME systems

A significant difference between older homes and today's tract houses is the **impressive and thoughtful** attention to the detailing inside. Homes of the past combined meticulous craftsmanship with functional space. While they may lack the closet space, number and size of windows, and two-story volume ceilings of their modern counterparts, the interiors of older homes were thoughtful of how folks lived then. Such consideration, I think, never goes out of style.

There are several reasons to restore your home's interior design and detailing. In addition to preserving the historic character of your home, repairing plaster walls and refinishing wood floors is generally less expensive than ripping them out and replacing them. Sure, there are systems that may need to be upgraded to meet today's standards for health, safety and the pursuit of high-tech living. But generally the materials used to build, finish and decorate your home's interior are of superior or equal quality to what's widely available today.

Renovating an older home is a delicate balancing act — incorporating the features desired for living in today's world while retaining the special details that make the home historic.

In this chapter, we'll go behind your walls and under your floors to see what's holding you together, then take a look at wall and floor finishes, windows and doors, trim and other detailing, all with a keen eye toward recognizing wear and deterioration and repairing the damage to preserve the original materials and finishes. Finally, we'll explore the various mechanical systems serving your house, including the plumbing, electrical and heating and cooling devices, and end with a discussion about energy efficiency that I think will be an eye-opener.

About your structure   Until the mid-1800s, homes were built like the barn-raising scene in the movie *Witness*, with multitudes of strong men crafting and lifting sections of wall and roof into place. For the floor structure, these post-and-beam homes used logs hewn (or shaped) on just one side to create a flat surface, while the remainder of the logs was left rounded. Wall studs, a standard structural element in modern building, were merely fillers for nailing the siding and plaster lath between the heavy timber posts, which were spaced several feet apart.

The introduction of the circular saw around 1840 changed the way homes were built; lumber could be mass-produced in smaller dimensions, making for lighter and therefore easier-to-construct members. In addition, the invention of cut nails and other fasteners helped speed the evolution of modern structural framing of floors, walls and roofs. These advancements also afforded architects the freedom to push the envelope with exterior bump-outs, various window placements and designs, and radius corners, adding character to a home's exterior.

Moving a nonload-bearing wall may require demolition, but repair usually can be accomplished less expensively than wholesale replacement.

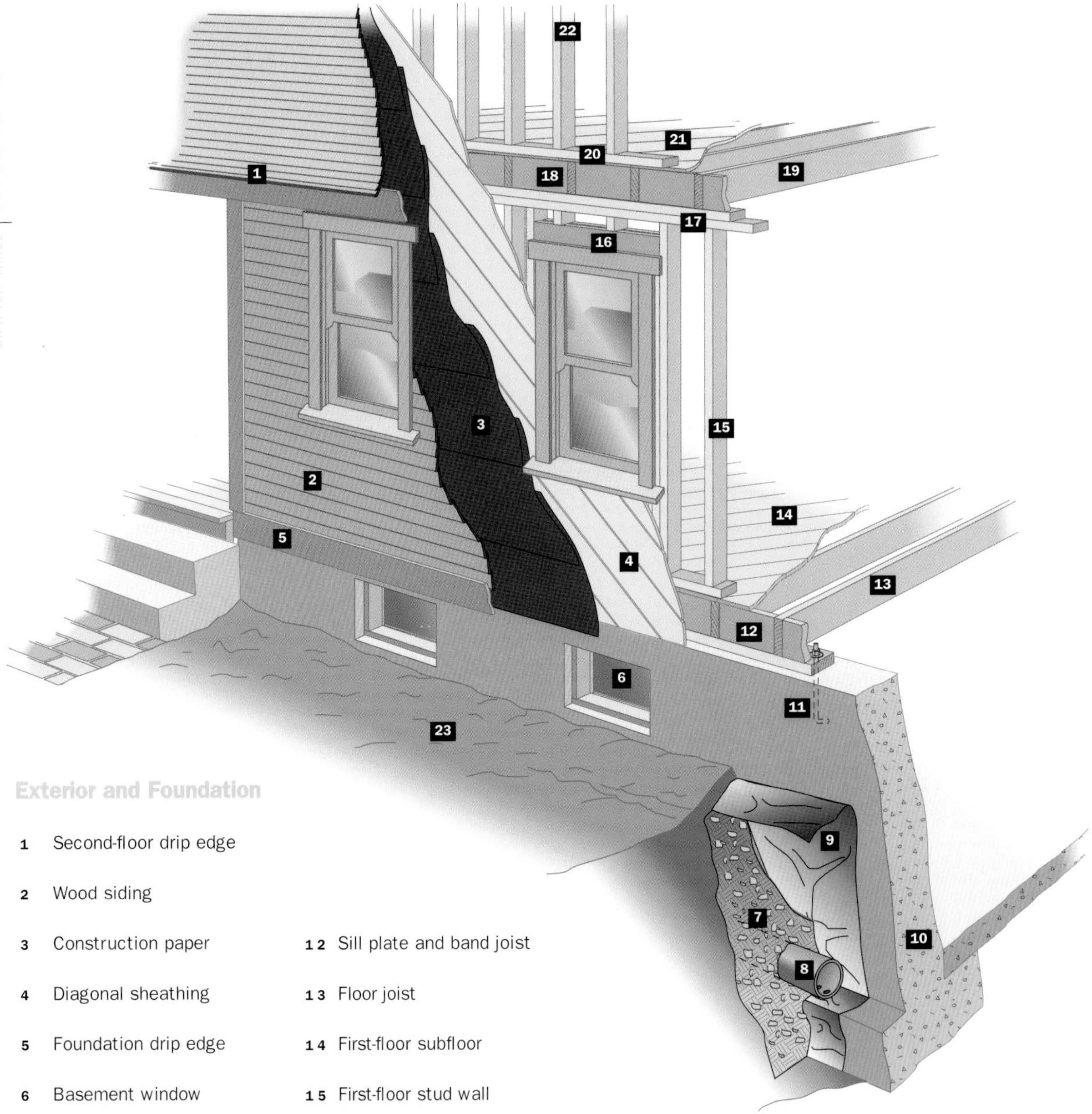

Exterior and Foundation

1   Second-floor drip edge

2   Wood siding

3   Construction paper

4   Diagonal sheathing

5   Foundation drip edge

6   Basement window

7   Drain gravel

8   Perforated drainpipe

9   Waterproof membrane

10 Foundation and footing

11 Foundation anchor bolt

12 Sill plate and band joist

13 Floor joist

14 First-floor subfloor

15 First-floor stud wall

16 Window header

17 First-floor cap

18 Second-floor band joist

19 Second-floor floor joist

20 Second-floor sill plate

21 Second-floor subfloor

22 Second-floor stud wall

23 Slope drains run-off
    water from foundation

If your home is 50 years or older, chances are it has what's called a balloon frame, meaning that the vertical posts and studs extend from the sill plate at the foundation to the top plate at the roof eaves, creating a continuous path for structural loads and resistance to wind and other natural elements. Because balloon framing uses long, continuous structural members, it was an easy transition for carpenters trained in the traditional post-and-beam method.

After World War II, the western, or platform, frame came into vogue, driven by the mass production of single-story homes in areas such as Levittown, New York, the Great Plains and Texas, and the Pacific Coast.

In platform framing, the vertical members extend only to the next floor or level; a two-story home, therefore, is really two framed structures, one on top of the other. The advantage of a platform frame is its simplicity, efficiency and strength: shorter pieces of lumber are lighter and easier to install, and their structural integrity is more reliable because of their shorter length. Homes could be built with less bracing and constructed in stages, with the platform protecting the frame below it while creating a work surface and staging area for the framing of the next level. With its single-level platform design, western framing mitigated the problems of balloon framing, which were its hollow cavity and lack of fire stops from the foundation to the roof.

It's important to know how your home's skeletal frame is constructed if you are to diagnose signs of wear and tear properly, since the proper remedies depend on how the various pieces of lumber are connected and work together.

Common problems include ceiling and floor joists that have sagged under heavy loads, especially if a second floor has been added or if the structure has been altered for a new opening or addition. Also, moisture damage or pest infestation may have caused lumber to deteriorate and lose its structural integrity. The soil underneath your house may have shifted or settled, pushing vertical members out of plumb (true vertical position), thereby making windows and doors stick or difficult to operate.

The first step before you begin to repair the damage is to determine the source of the problem and fix it. Be consoled that large timbers (especially those milled from stronger, old-growth timber) and even smaller-dimension lumber may have deteriorated without necessarily losing a lot of strength; it really depends on where the wear is, what the lumber is holding up and how extensive the damage is (even charred wood still may be useful).

Many of the moisture-related causes, such as poor drainage and excessive runoff, are covered in Chapter Two. To take sag out of a roof or floor may require you to replace the structural members or simply jack up the affected area and sister a section of lumber onto the side of the existing roof rafter or floor joist to help carry the load above. However, if weight and time have pushed your vertical walls out of plumb, you'll likely need more complicated, professional techniques, like house jacking. A thorough inspection of the structure prior to purchasing the house or beginning any restoration work will provide the diagnosis and options for restoring the structure to its original form and integrity.

Water damage, caused by such as this roof leak, is sometimes obvious, other times not. The most insidious moisture is water vapor trapped within interior walls due to inadequate ventilation of appliances, kitchens and bathrooms.

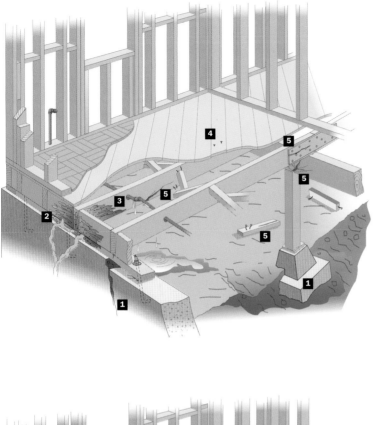

Problems with a floor may result from many causes: (1) settling foundations, (2) insect infestation or fungal infection, (3) leaking plumbing, (4) loose fasteners between floor, subfloor and joists, and (5) cracked, broken or missing support timbers, joists and cross-braces.

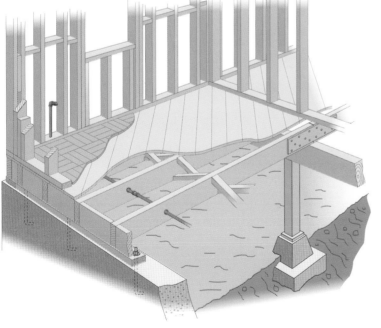

After repairing all defects, the floor is level and well-supported. All infested and damaged wood was treated, removed or replaced, both plumbing and foundation were repaired to eliminate the cause of settling, and the flooring was renailed to stop squeaks.

Doors and windows   No house, old or new, is perfectly square and true, but if the structure of your older home is stable and has been maintained properly, you can turn your attention to the doors, windows and plaster, which are affected directly by the "rightness" of the home's structural frame.

Doors and windows offer a fascinating look at the evolution of home design and product technology. Early batten-type doors, with their simple construction but vulnerability to changing climates; window glass with bubbles and a wavy appearance, indicating that's how it was manufactured; and, finally, period panel doors and double-hung windows, which improved functionality on several levels and opened up myriad design possibilities.

Panel doors were developed in the 1700s as an alternative to batten doors, which could not combat the effects of moisture and climate changes on their operation. Combining several, smaller components (stiles, rails and loose-fitting panels) into a single structure allowed the door to maintain its shape, expanding and contracting (as wood will) within an acceptable tolerance. (If you have true panel doors in your old home that stick or won't close, check the squareness of the opening before you plane down the door.)

If your house has old panel doors, they're worth restoring because they evolved into showpieces for a craftsman's woodworking skills. The result was detailed center panels that matched the baseboards, cornices, mantelpieces and cabinetry of a specific room or rooms throughout the house.

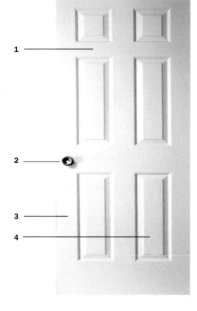

Components of a typical modern panel door:

1 STILE

2 HARDWARE: LOCK SET AND HINGES

3 RAIL

4 PANEL

Like all home features, panel doors are subject to the effects of use and abuse —
dents and dings, loose hardware and hinges, and separation of the components at
their joint connections. Several products and methods exist to restore panel
doors. Paintable wood and epoxy fillers will repair dents; longer screws can
secure hinges back to the door jamb; clamps, glue and concealed fasteners and
dowels will repair joints. A tasteful brass toe kick will guard against future damage.
And because the panels are set loose in the door's frame, damaged sections can
be removed, then replicated or repaired by any woodworker worth his salt. Only
as a last resort should you plane down a stile or rail to fix a panel door. [See
Chapter One for the value and availability of salvaged or reproduction hardware
for doors, windows and other historic elements.]

Like doors, windows have their own history, evolving from small holes in the
wall that helped ventilate the house and let in light to multifunctional designs
in a variety of shapes and sizes. Windows really came into their own in the late
1800s with advances in glass technology and companion changes in frame
construction, both of which allowed for a freer use of windows to capture views,
provide even better ventilation and shape the exterior design.

The first operable windows were casement, or out-swing, types, which were
placed strategically to direct prevailing breezes into the house. A simple crank
made it possible to regulate the amount and flow of air, while screens mounted
on the inside of the window frame kept out pests and debris.

Restoration of old panel
doors entails much work,
but the results are dramatic.

Double-hung windows in historic homes have clever counterweight systems of ropes, pulleys and heavy sash weights that balance the window when open.

Later, sash (or hung) windows were developed, first with only one operable sash (the bottom one), then with both sashes operable to vent hot air out the top while enticing breezes through the bottom. An ingenious system of counterweights and pulleys regulated the window operation, holding the sashes in any position. Concealed in the sash frame and the window jamb (or frame), so-called pocket doors and plates provided access to the weights and pulleys should they need repair. Unless your window sashes have deteriorated beyond fixing, this design is still effective and worth preserving.

Because they involve movable pieces and frequent use, windows (like doors) will eventually show signs of wear; because they also are subject to the elements, windows can suffer from moisture damage, insect infestation and the wrath of the weather.

A telltale sign of a window's condition is the state of the paint, especially on the horizontal surfaces and joints, such as at the sill. Paint will not adhere well to a moist surface nor one that has moisture trapped within it.

Once you've found and corrected the source of the moisture, you'll want to repair the window.

Proper window maintenance may then include periodic paint removal, reglazing, repairing with epoxy or fillers, weatherstripping the sashes and repainting. Even a badly damaged sill may be reparable with the right mix of compounds, which can be used to build up missing or damaged sections, then sanded and painted to appear like new.

Another common problem I see with older windows is the deterioration of the glazing putty, which helps hold the glass in place and sheds water away from the wood frame. Worn by freeze-thaw cycles and sunlight, the putty can become dry and cracked, eventually losing its adhesive qualities.

Fortunately, reglazing is simple with modern putty compounds that far outlast their precursors. Once the window sash is removed, the original putty can be scraped off, the glazier's points (the small metal inserts that hold the glass in place) removed and the wood sanded and cleaned; I recommend a 50:50 solution of boiled linseed oil and denatured alcohol, which will help preserve the wood. A clean glass and frame will adhere to the new putty and provide a perimeter seal to the outside elements.

As you reglaze the window sash, you may be tempted to swap insulated glass for the original, single-pane glazing. Insulated glass, a combination of two panels of glass separated by air and sealed together, is necessary for a glass-walled skyscraper but provides little energy savings for a home; at perhaps four times the price it's not a cost-efficient choice either. As a rule of restoration, I always try to keep the original windows as they are, even with their single-pane glass, rather than swapping them for upgraded units. A tight, well-made wood storm window will perform as well as a double-glazed window and, of course, is more historically correct.

In addition to providing extra insulation, storm windows help protect your old, wood-frame windows by relieving them of having to brave the weather. Storms

Peeling paint on a window often results from moisture sneaking past storm windows into cracks in the exterior paint or from interior condensation dripping down the glass glazing. Care taken in sealing and painting will cure the former; installing a tight, well-made storm window will help the latter.

Any complete window replacement requires breaking into the exterior shell of the home. Here, the window frame moldings and some sill trim have been removed partially, and a salvaged window has been inserted into the opening.

Replacing windows

Let's say that due to severe damage or deterioration your old windows need to be replaced. You have some choices to make, especially if you are going to preserve the integrity of your home's design and exterior.

Of primary consideration are the sizes, shapes, design, details, operation and frame material of your windows, the latter of which most likely will be wood. A wood-frame window can be an efficient, long-lasting product with proper maintenance. It is thermally superior to synthetic alternatives, and it's made from a renewable natural resource. In addition, today's glazing technology, including new energy-efficient glass and gasketing, makes these windows even more efficient and practical.

It's tempting to dream up new and dramatic window designs given the variety of product available these days. But because of the care taken in the original placement and design of your home's windows, any changes would violate the historic integrity of the home and likely its performance. You may want that Palladian window or skylight for your upstairs master bedroom, but my advice is to save it for a tasteful addition or simply move into a newer house with such features.

also add another design element to the exterior and can be fitted with removable panels for glass or screens, depending on the season.

To say that I prefer wood storm windows to aluminum is, at best, an understatement. In short, I will never put aluminum storms on my windows or doors for the simple reason that, by nature, they conduct heat and cold. Condensation forms on the inside panes, which then drips down to the window and door sills, causing moisture damage. Wood-framed storm windows, on the other hand, insulate against heat and cold.

A few tips: When you install a storm over an existing window, make sure its center rail aligns with the center sash connection of the window. That way, the storm appears virtually invisible and allows the window to ventilate properly when the storm is set. Also, leave a slight gap (about $\frac{1}{8}$ inch) between the storm and the window sill to help ventilate any moisture that may form between the two units. Finally, modern wood storms should have high-density foam or neoprene weatherstripping on the top and sides of the frame and a full-size, permanent screen that extends to the outside edges; the inside edges accommodate glass inserts that can be removed from inside the house.

About plaster   While it may seem obvious at this point why you should do your best to restore and preserve your original doors and windows, perhaps less obvious are the reasons to maintain your home's original lath and plaster walls. To the untrained or uninformed eye, they just look like something to hold the paint, wallpaper and family photographs.

Not so. Like most parts of an older home, the plaster was the work of a skilled tradesman. Even the construction of early lath required skill and craftsmanship. A panel of thin-dimension wood was sliced horizontally to resemble an accordion, then stretched out to reveal the gaps that would accept the first, or scratch, coat of plaster. [See the modern equivalent of this process in the illustration on the following page.]

A lath and plaster wall is the most durable, versatile and easy-to-maintain wall you can have. It was applied over brick, stone or wood wall construction, providing a solid barrier to fire and sound. It also is very workable, able to be shaped around corners and radius walls and finished with wallpaper, paint, stenciling, texturing or many other types of decorative treatments. Only the economics of its content and construction drove it from the home-building industry in favor of sheet drywall and paneling.

To appreciate fully plaster's value, you have to understand its four-stage application process, beginning with the lath. Initially, lath was wood, which typically was soaked with water so as not to draw moisture from the wet plaster coats. Wood lath was followed by rock-lath panel, then steel-lath materials, all fastened similarly to the wall frame.

Once the lath was set, the plasterer would apply the scratch coat, pressing it between the slats in the lath so that the plaster oozed out behind it, securing it to the lath once dry (called keying). The scratch coat was then abraded or scratched up to create a surface that would accept and hold the thicker base

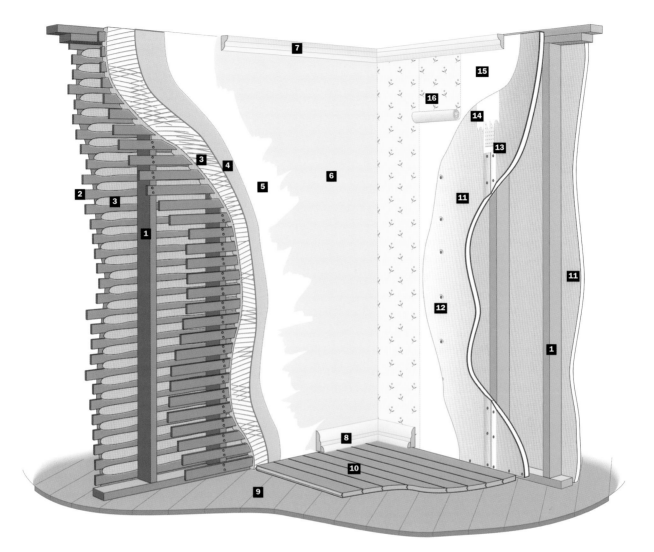

Interior Walls

1. Studwall, sill plate and header

2. Wooden lath

3. Plaster scratch coat and "keys" holding it to lath

4. Plaster brown coat

5. Plaster top coat

6. Sealer and paint

7. Crown molding

8. Baseboard molding

9. Diagonally laid subfloor

10. Tongue and groove solid oak flooring

11. Drywall board

12. Drywall fasteners

13. Joint or seam tape

14. joint compound

15. Skim or "Cal" coat

16. Wallpaper or wallcovering

(or brown) coat. Rough textured by composition, the brown coat provided the thickness of the wall and accepted the finish or top coat, often a smoother, thinner layer resembling the scratch coat. Mind you, each of these layers had a specific mixture of natural elements, including sand, crushed oyster shells and animal hair, usually horse, cow or hog. If each was not mixed properly, the plaster would lose its ability to adhere to the lath or other layers, causing it to disintegrate, crack, flake or fall off in chunks.

Early versions of plaster could take up to a year to cure before paint or wallpaper could be applied to the surface. Building lore tells of old-time plasterers who would test a wall's dryness by striking a match on the unfinished top coat; if the match lit, the wall was ready to finish. Newer compounds, including the joint compound typically recommended to repair plaster cracks today, dry much faster.

Of course, plaster isn't perfect; as an organic material, it will deteriorate under heavy loads and is vulnerable to moisture infiltration. If you have an aging plaster ceiling, a sag likely indicates that the plaster keys have broken off behind the lath from simple gravity. Specially designed screws and washers can resecure the plaster to the framing, eliminating the sag without requiring replacement of the falling section.

In addition to gravitational pull, structural problems can affect plaster. Forces pushing against a wall can create diagonal cracks that often start at door and window openings, where the wall is unable to move as freely. These are usually due to deflection in the ceiling frame or joists, which push down on the plaster, causing it to crack or sag, or to expansive soil conditions, which may have

The scratch coat of plaster, here many years old and revealed in the process of demolition, still adheres strongly to the wooden lath.

allowed the house to settle. Small (if chronic) cracks may signal a wood lath reacting to changes in moisture or climate.

For deep or large cracks or missing sections of plaster, be sure to remove all loose pieces thoroughly and clean the exposed plaster and lath with a TSP or other cleaning solution produced for such a purpose. You may want to attach new metal lath over the old wood lath in the affected section, which will help to inhibit cracking in the future. Finally, the old plaster layers should be stepped down to help the new coats adhere to them.

Small, hairline cracks are of little consequence to the structural integrity of the plaster, but if you find them unsightly, you probably can take on the task of repairing them yourself. First, you'll have to dig them out a bit to create enough of a surface to hold a compound of siliconized latex or plaster filler, the former of which will remain flexible inside the crack; you also might want to install a small section of fiberglass tape along the length of the crack to bridge it and thus keep it from resurfacing.

Flexing in the structural support members of this staircase weakened the plaster on this wall until it failed under the stress.

A word to the wise: Even simple patching of plaster and plaster of Paris requires a lime additive to work effectively, so make sure whatever compounds you buy contain it.

Now, all that being said, when we began restoring our house in Rock Island, Illinois, several walls were cluttered with small cracks. But instead of digging out all these little fissures to fill them, I employed a new process that employs an ingenious fiberglass fabric system.

First, a vinyl coating, like thick paint, is rolled over the wall section you want to repair. Then, fabric is laid directly onto the coating and, like wallpaper, is cut around the trim, light fixtures and windows. The combination of materials bridges the wall to mitigate cracks in the future and creates an effective vapor barrier to prevent warm, moist air from getting into the wall cavity if the outside wall or cavity is insulated (discussed in Chapter Two). Finally, it provides a smooth, plasterlike wall to finish.

About trim and finishes Now that we've dealt with the interior structure of the house, it's time to get down to the details: the woodwork, wallpaper, paint, tile, decorative plaster and flooring materials that personalize your home's interior character.

The biggest concern about removing, repairing or restoring old finishes is that you never know what you might uncover or damage unwittingly in the process. Unless your home is a few hundred years old, chances are you won't see early paints such as whitewash, linseed oil or caesin (milk-based); it's also unlikely you'll recover the precious, imported, handmade wallpaper of the 1700s. But you may reveal remnants of a painted mural behind layers of wallpaper, or a pine substrate behind a column painted to look like oak, since paint treatments that replicated more expensive materials were common before the 1930s. What this all means is that such restoration projects should be a slow-moving train to allow you to discover and appreciate the interior changes your home has experienced throughout its history and reclaim what you can.

About drywall   I love real lath and plaster, but I also like drywall. It is made from gypsum powder pressed and molded into panels ranging in thicknesses up to $\frac{3}{4}$ inch and overall dimensions of 4x8 feet, 4x10 feet and 4x12 feet (the larger the panel, the fewer the seams on a wall). Commercial-grade drywall also is a better barrier to sound and fire than is plaster.

For homes that are not landmark quality and in which the original plaster walls and ceilings are damaged beyond repair, installing (or hanging) drywall is an adequate and less-expensive solution than replastering. In addition, gutting a wall to its frame to install drywall means upgrading plumbing, electrical and HVAC systems in the wall or ceiling cavities, which will cost about the same as if it was new construction and up to 60 percent less than if you had to snake various pipes and wires behind an existing plaster wall. If the job is done right, most homeowners can't tell the difference.

A quality drywall job involves the contractor installing $\frac{5}{8}$ inch panels, carefully taping all of the joints (or seams) and concealing countersunk screw heads with joint compound. A smooth skim coat, usually about $\frac{1}{8}$ inch thick (sometimes called cal coating), will resemble most closely the original plaster.

Drywall panels were developed after World War II to meet the burgeoning demand for single-family housing during the baby boom years. These panels quickly replaced lath and plaster because they installed in a fraction of the time and finished to a uniform smoothness. What they lacked in charm and durability they more than made up for in convenience and cost savings.

If you're going to the trouble of tearing out, replacing and finishing a wall or damaged section but have budget limitations, consider rock lath, an acceptable hybrid between drywall and plaster. These gypsum panels have a coating that combines the lath and scratch coat into a single step and accepts the brown coat, reducing your installation by a quarter. While I like this option for its historic merits, it isn't as economical as a good-quality drywall job.

Painted wood   I'll never forget touring an original 1929 Sears kit house several years back. The home was charming, complete with a banister that had to be notched so an in-swing window could open over it and a mosaic tile floor that had a slight imperfection created intentionally so as not to offend God (no kidding). I recall commenting to the owner about the beautiful exposed wood columns, trim and floor; she replied that, in fact, back in the '20s, such raw wood exposure was a sign of poverty and that painted surfaces, in turn, signified wealth. While her treatment of the details may not have been accurate to the period of the home, they were a statement about how today's perceptions of value have changed.

Identifying interior paint in need of repair, whether on your walls or trim, follows the same rules as paint applied to the exterior: if it's peeling, cracking, abraded or flaking, it has been affected by moisture, sunlight, soil or dirt and soot generated by various household appliances.

Less known but nonetheless common is damage caused by a stronger paint, like an oil-based or alkyd, that has been applied over a weaker paint, such as a water-based or latex. The stronger paint peels away from the weaker finish, which may, in turn, be peeling off the substrate. So remember: latex can go over oil, but not the other way around.

But the primary culprit, as always, is moisture, both as water and vapor. We've addressed water infiltration in Chapter Two; to help control interior vapor, properly ventilate areas where moisture is generated, such as kitchens and bathrooms, and keep the relative humidity inside your house to about 40 percent (drier could be unhealthy). Newer thermostats are equipped with a humidity meter; you can regulate the level in your home by using exhaust fans in the bathrooms, limiting the number of indoor plants and venting appliances.

There are several ways to strip off old paint, lacquer, shellac and wallpaper; I prefer gentler methods, such as environmentally safe chemical and organic strippers, as opposed to heat guns and abrasives. Denatured alcohol and other chemical compounds can be effective methods for lifting off old surfaces, especially from wood. All you need then is a set of scrapers, awls, toothbrushes and rags to help

The finest homes always include decorative touches to finish ceilings and walls. Crown moldings (top) and cast plaster medallions (bottom) are easy to install.

you get into those tiny cracks and crevices without damaging the detail. The goal is to maintain the original finishes whenever possible; think about these details the way you would a valuable piece of antique furniture — if you remove the original finish, the piece has lost most of its value.

Like paint, wallpaper reacts poorly to moisture, and, until recently, standard practice was simply to cover it with new paper or paint. But stripping is essential to restoring the wall and the room to its original design because if you uncover a remnant of the initial treatment it will tell you if the wall was originally intended to be painted or papered.

Depending on the style and age of your older home, it may include some very intricate detailing, such as plaster crown moldings, coffered ceilings, chair rails, finely detailed mantels and built-in cabinetry; less dramatic but no less important detailing includes the baseboard trim, ceramic tile inlays and the width, construction and finish of the wood flooring.

To repair and replicate historic plaster molding, skilled plasterers of today, like their predecessors, will carefully mix the compounds, create the molds and stencils, and shape and style any intricate details with a unique set of tools. While some modern home builders will offer to replicate a coffered or tray ceiling or build up layers of wood trim pieces to create a crown molding, there's definitely something special and timeless about watching a craftsman draw his precut running mold along the wall-ceiling joint, building up a deep plaster cornice with each pass.

About your flooring Because of its abundance in the early part of our country's building history, wood provided a durable, inexpensive material for a variety of applications, including floors. First hewn from logs as wide, tapered planks (a significant detail to remember if you need to replace a plank or two), wood flooring evolved to feature concealed spline-and-groove connectors, shiplap and tongue-and-groove installation, and inlaid and parquet detailing.

While the beauty of natural wood floors may be of high value today, in the past, not all were meant to be seen; in fact, many softer woods were painted to replicate a hardwood, such as oak or cherry.

Refinishing a wood floor is not only cheaper than covering it with wall-to-wall carpeting, it's truer to your home's history. For most jobs, I recommend a passive approach, such as a deep cleaning and light sanding of stained areas. More aggressive measures, such as sanding a wood floor down to its bare surface, will destroy evidence of the home's progression through history.

Replacing planks or sections of an old wood floor used to be problematic. However, recently a number of wood floor remanufacturers have sprung up who purchase salvaged timbers from dilapidated or destroyed warehouses and industrial buildings, remove all the fasteners and connectors and mill the pieces down to plank wood flooring. The process is the ultimate in recycling and provides a supply of truly historic (if more expensive) flooring material for restoration projects.

Preserving and restoring historic parquet floors is a bit trickier and time-consuming. Originally, the pieces of these intricately designed floors were laid on

The glory of natural wood flooring is revealed through careful cleaning, light sanding, repair of any damage and a new finish.

a canvas backing, then the entire floor or the border was inlaid with small fasteners. Parquet floors can suffer from simple wear to popped nails to buckling caused by moisture infiltration. By design, it is more difficult to repair a parquet floor than to build a new one because it often requires replicating and replacing small, damaged sections. To refinish them, I recommend gentle chemical strippers and cleaners because sanding may wear the thin parquet down to its base or even through to the subfloor.

Whether planks or parquet, pine or oak, I urge you to finish your wood floors with coats of satin polyurethane or a Danish (tongue-oil) finish. Doing so reveals the beauty of the wood as well as its grains and contours.

Some exceptional homes have inlaid floors — intricate patterns of wood using different grains, colors and even species of trees — to create geometric designs and borders around the edges or in the center of the floor.

There are other kinds of flooring, of course, each with its own history in interior design. In older homes, it isn't uncommon to come across true linoleum flooring, though it usually is unreclaimable. Linoleum, initially an organic, durable combination of linseed oil, rosin, wood flour, cork powder, natural pigments and mildew inhibitors over a jute, canvas or felt backing, evolved into today's vinyl sheet and tile flooring.

Most commonly used in today's kitchens, bathrooms and laundry areas, modern vinyl flooring is available in hundreds of patterns and styles, including faux plank wood and ceramic tile designs. The primary rule of thumb: the thicker the vinyl on the wear side, the better quality the material.

A technique I recommend for replacing a worn linoleum or vinyl floor is to leave any undamaged sections in place, remove all the loose tiles or damaged sections,

fill the voids with a flooring putty, sand the entire surface to an even level, then glue and nail a sheet of $\frac{1}{4}$-to-$\frac{3}{8}$-inch clear plywood or oriented strand board over the whole area. Doing so relieves you of having to pry up the old material while providing you with a flat, smooth surface ready for new vinyl sheet or tile. A threshold between the new floor and an adjacent flooring material will ease the transition.

Ceramic tile has its roots in ancient times; its popularity throughout history is a testament to its durability and versatility. Appropriate for inside and outside use, on floors and walls, it can be molded, shaped, pigmented, carved and inlaid to create unique patterns and styles.

In the past, tile floors were laid over a thick bed of cementitious mortar and required additional support from the frame below. (If your tile floor sags or slopes, it may be due to undersized floor joists). Today, especially on countertops and tub and shower walls, tile is laid on a $\frac{3}{8}$-to-$\frac{5}{8}$-inch thick cement board, commonly referred to by a brand name, Durock™, which is set on a much thinner bed of high-strength, moisture-resistant adhesive mortar.

Tile, while durable, is not indestructible. Damage usually isn't from overuse but from some sort of impact (like a dropped hair dryer) or moisture and mildew infiltration that have worn away the grout, leaving the tile vulnerable to cracking and chipping.

Fortunately, the historic popularity of ceramic tile may allow you to match a missing or damaged piece or section closely. Bring a piece of your damaged

1 Controlling humidity in a typical home may involve balancing the house's **HVAC** system — heating, ventilating and air conditioning — to add or remove moisture while maintaining a comfortable room temperature.

2 Squeaks usually are easy to fix: a lag screw will bind the flooring to the underlying support joist. When squeaks result from settling, rot or insect infestation, however, the only solution may be to replace the defective piece with new wood.

3 Many houses have a variety of flooring types. When considering floor renovations, a retail showroom is the smartest place to explore the choices.

4 Options for formal areas include marble (shown here in contrasting black and white tiles), granite, slate, wood and other materials, including vinyl, ceramic tile or wall-to-wall carpeting.

tile to a local supplier to find the best (or perfect) match, but if you can't, don't give up hope. There are several local, national and international tile manufacturers and suppliers who specialize in historic remnants. The only difference may be in contour, dimension, glaze or shading.

The most common repair for ceramic tile is actually for the grout, which should be checked as part of your annual home maintenance. If the grout is cracking, chipping or has sections missing, it should be cleaned out thoroughly and replaced with new grout, available at most hardware stores and home centers. If your grout is colored (or pigmented), take a sample to a dedicated tile center, which is likely to have more variety and expertise than a home center in helping to match it with the original.

Ceramic tile and pavers are offered in a wide variety of colors and textures.

The advent of wall-to-wall carpeting coincided with our nation's first housing boom back in the '20s, when folks thought covering up their bare wood finishes was a sign of wealth. Today, for practical if not historical reasons, carpeting rivals wood as a desired floor covering, especially in living rooms and bedrooms.

If your restoration project calls for new carpeting, look into the myriad wholesale manufacturers who offer their carpeting direct from the factory (Dalton, Georgia, is mecca for carpet making). These companies recently have made carpeting available to homeowners at wholesale prices. They may even provide a list of installers in your area who do not require that you purchase carpet from them. These suppliers will send you sample books with a variety of wools and olifin-nylon blends in numerous patterns, textures and colors. (Look for their ads in the classified section of your favorite home improvement magazine.)

Underlying the wide variety of colors, textures and patterns available in today's carpeting is the range of quality. In short, the thicker the weave the better; carpet also is rated by weight, the heavier the better. Finally, for the most durable material, look to wools or olifin-nylon blends instead of strictly nylon carpeting. While they can't be dyed easily, they naturally resist stains.

About your mechanical systems Behind your walls, under your floors and in your ceilings exists an intricate web of wires, pipes, conduits and ducts that service the rooms of your home with electricity, water, waste disposal, ventilation, natural gas and heat. Before buying an older home, you need to make sure these systems either have been added to or upgraded to meet occupant demands and current building codes for heath and safety.

The late 1800s is generally regarded as the beginning of modern home building; both electricity and indoor plumbing were invented and popularized during that time, forever changing the American home. Even as early as 1893, with the first edition of the National Energy Code, respect for these technologies was acknowledged by the home-building industry.

Early electrical systems, commonly known as knob and tube wiring because cloth-insulated wires were connected to each other through porcelain insulators, soon became inadequate (and unsafe — as the cloth wore away, the bare wires

Wall-to-wall carpeting is sold by the square yard: to estimate the amount you will need, divide the room's square footage by 9.

were left exposed) for the rush of new, electric appliances and products. Eventually, electricity was regulated by a central fuse box and subpanels that serviced distinct areas of electrical demand. But even this system, with plastic-insulated wiring, could burn out if overloaded, posing a fire hazard.

Today, the fuses and runs of individual wires have been replaced by circuit breakers and coated bundles of wire (called Romex™), with circuit panels that can be upgraded to accommodate the demands of computers, security systems, entertainment equipment and the variety of small appliances we require in our homes today. Even homes built as recently as the early 1980s may require upgrades; from the 1960s until the mid-'80s, 100-amp service was adequate, but the proliferation of home computers and other electrical equipment has pushed the norm to 200-amp service in new homes.

Plumbing systems, too, have evolved greatly since the turn of the century. Without the benefit of today's municipal water sources, early versions of indoor plumbing were controlled by a pump-driven, pressurized tank in the basement; a series of valves released water to the system, while air pressure at the top of the tank drove the water to the source. The problem was that the system allowed sewer gasses from the various fixtures to flow back into the house.

Eventually, concern for sewer gas emissions led to the development of the vent stack, a waste-and-gas-disposal pipe that extended from the basement (or lowest floor) to the roof. Traps were designed into the plumbing fixtures to hold water, which would then block sewer gasses from entering the room. Early vent stacks

Central fuses and knob and tube wiring — also known as pillar and post — were standard when homes were first electrified. Today, they have been replaced by circuit breakers and cabled wire in most residential construction.

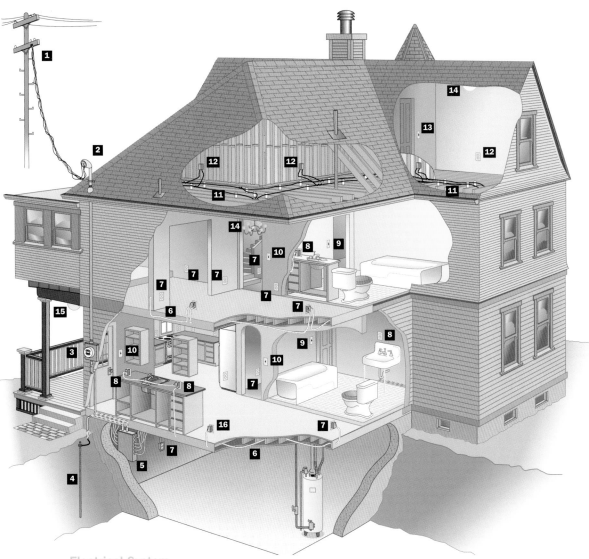

Electrical System

1 Utility Power Connection

2 House 220 Volt Electric
   Service Entrance

3 Utility Electric Meter

4 Primary Grounding Stake

5 Electrical Main Box with
   Circuit Breakers and
   Multiple Circuits

6 110 Volt Romex® Cable
   Wiring Circuit

7 Grounded Outlets

8 Ground Fault Protected
   Outlets

9 Ground Fault Protected
   Light Switches

10 Grounded Light Switches

11 Obsolete Knob & Tube
    Wiring Circuit

12 Ungrounded Outlets

13 Ungrounded Switches

14 Interior Lighting Fixtures

15 Weatherproof Exterior
    Lighting Fixtures

16 220 Volt Outlet

Galvanized pipe Galvanized, or
zinc-coated, pipe was once the
material of choice for early plumbing
systems. However, galvanized pipe
can collect mineral buildup from the
water system, causing it to clog
and thereby reduce water pressure.

The fix? The first step is to clean out
the gunk that has collected. Next,
inspect the pipes for buildup, which
may be so bad as to have reduced a
¾-inch pipe to a pinhole. If that's the
case, you're looking at replacement,
usually to copper, which can last
80 years or more. If the buildup is
minimal, try over-the-counter solutions
to help clean it out.

When replacing galvanized pipe
with copper, be sure to correct for
galvanic current, the electrical
reaction that occurs when two
dissimilar metals connect, by using
either brass or insulated fittings.

were made from cast iron; today's newer technology uses lightweight plastic
(either ABS or PVC) in place of its cumbersome precursor.

Iron pipes are frequently in fine working order in older homes. However, if
you need to replace worn or broken sections, keep in mind that many early
pipes were manufactured to nonstandard dimensions, which can make them
difficult to match with modern sizes. While cast iron pipe and fittings are
readily available today, before removing any section of an old cast iron pipe,
fitting, washer or other part of the system, make sure you can find a comparably
sized replacement piece.

With both plumbing and electrical systems, remember that upgrades can intrude
on the interior design or require removal of original wall surfaces and finishes. To
maintain your walls in their original state, find existing chases or interior soffits in
which to install any upgraded systems. Fortunately, the parts and pieces of modern
plumbing and electrical systems typically are smaller than their predecessors',
meaning you should be able to accommodate them easily.

Installing a heating, ventilating and air conditioning (or HVAC) system entails
a few more concerns, however. The first central heating systems came into use in
the early nineteenth century with the original wood- and coal-fired furnaces,
which included ductwork to deliver heat to the various rooms of the house. By
contrast, early steam systems, similar to the early plumbing systems, delivered
heat through small-diameter pipes to room radiators. (By the end of the century,
hot water replaced steam as a safer, more controllable option.)

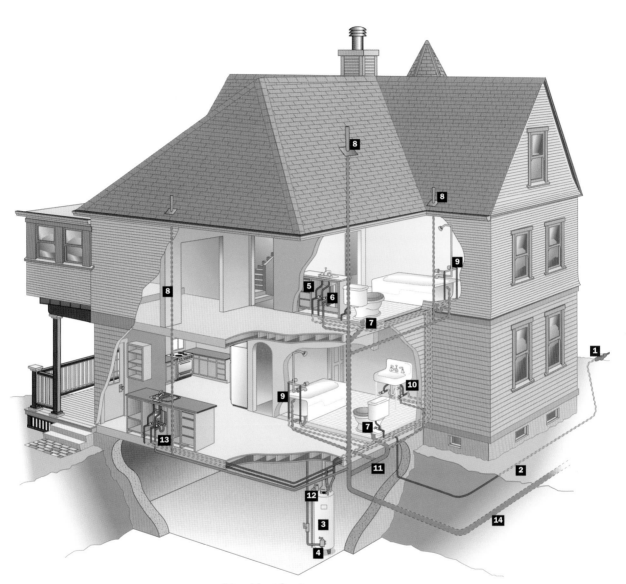

Plumbing Systems

1	Water service meter	8	Wastewater vent stack
2	Water service line	9	Tub and shower service
3	Water heater	10	Sink service
4	Gas or electric igniter	11	Sewer waste junction
5	Cold water supply line	12	Pressure relief valve
6	Hot water supply line	13	Garbage disposal
7	Toilet	14	Main sewer outflow line

Early wood- and coal-fired gravity furnaces may look monstrous and inefficient, but, in fact, they have proven quite adequate for gas conversion. Made from heavy-gauge steel and lined with brick, these furnaces continue radiating heat after they shut off, saving on energy costs. And, if they do need replacing, their huge ducts conveniently provide chases for new, modern ductwork.

To bring HVAC to all levels of your old house, consider a two-zone (or area) system, with a separate appliance in the attic that utilizes ceiling vents and port-holes to serve the second-floor rooms. This design is especially pertinent if your old house has a boiler or radiant heating system in the basement, which provides no ductwork or chases through the walls but rather heats the home through small, pressurized pipes to room radiators.

Because heat rises and will filter up to a second floor, I generally install a separate cooling system for that floor only if it is 1,200 square feet or larger. For instance, I'll install the cooling unit in the attic and spot vents for the ductwork in the ceiling below so the forced, cool air will filter down into the room.

Even if you have a system that serves all levels of your house, there are a few tricks of the trade that will help regulate the distribution of heat throughout the entire structure.

Keeping the dynamics of heat transfer in mind, to control rising heat you'll want to adjust the vent registers on the upper levels to a nearly closed position and use ceiling fans on a low setting to circulate the air; below, leave the vents and any closures to staircases wide open to allow the warm air to rise naturally.

No matter how many cold winters this ancient boiler may have endured, its day is probably long past; energy-efficiency improvements will pay back the owner, and valuable space will become available for use. Be sure to consider keeping the existing ducts and pipe work, if it is possible in your situation.

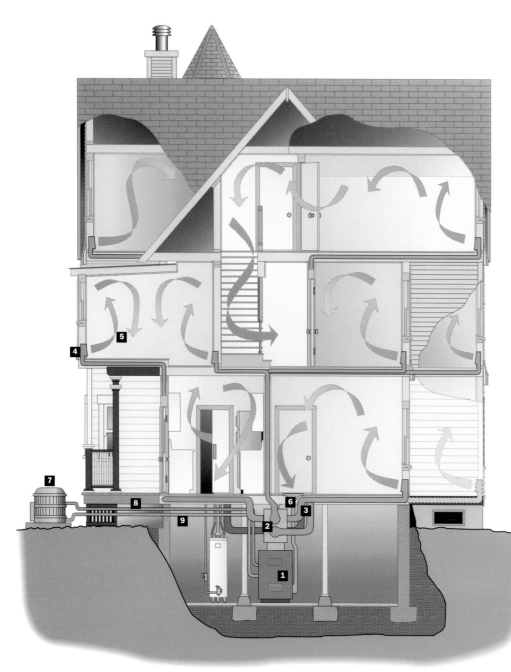

A nonzoned heating, ventilating and air conditioning system

1 Oil- or gas-fueled furnace with heat exchanger and air filter

2 Plenum mixing chamber

3 Warm (heat) or cool (air conditioning) feed ducts

4 Air control register

5 Warm air circulation flow

6 Cool-air-return supply vent

7 Compressor-condenser for air conditioning

8 Warm evaporate feed line

9 Cold condensate return line

About insulation and energy efficiency With all the attention paid today to energy efficiency and conservation, the market has become flooded with products and gizmos that allegedly provide energy upgrades to older homes. However, a government study found that homes built *before* 1940 and *after* 1975 are more energy efficient than those built in-between.

How can that be? Simply, homes built before the baby boom were naturally designed to accommodate their energy needs. Operable windows (strategically placed to provide light and ventilation), interior transoms, masonry fireplaces and plaster walls all played functional roles in helping control heat transfer and circulate hot and cool air throughout the house. Insulation, if any, was newspaper or sawdust in the attic or loosely mortared brick in the sidewalls. Instead, covered porches, deep roof overhangs, awnings and even dark exterior paint colors ingeniously provided shade from the sun and kept heat gain to a minimum. Trees were planted to provide windbreaks and shade in the summer; in the winter, their bare branches allowed sunlight and heat into the house.

What is it? A box sill — the short, framed sidewall that extends from the top of the house's foundation to the joists of the first floor — and a prime candidate for insulation with glass fiber and foam to prevent high energy bills. An added vapor barrier of plastic would complete the installation.

With these existing, if passive, systems in place, upgrades to weatherize and tighten older homes can be kept to a minimum, which not only will save on restoration costs but will maintain your home's historic character. (If you own one of those energy hogs from the middle part of the century, you still should take care to incorporate only the most effective methods for achieving better energy efficiency.)

First, take additional passive measures to reduce energy use. Set the thermostat to moderate levels, such as 68 degrees in the winter and 78 degrees in the summer, and have your HVAC system checked annually to optimize its performance. Also, close registers in infrequently used or seasonal rooms and employ operable windows and other ventilation features. Alone, these measures can reduce energy use by up to 30 percent, with attendant cost savings.

More aggressive measures, including upgrading HVAC equipment or installing new insulation, should be weighed carefully against their real cost savings and the impact on the home's interior and exterior structure and design elements. For example, simply caulking and weatherstripping around doors, windows and service outlets on exterior walls, installing and properly maintaining storm windows and doors (detailed earlier in this chapter) and adding a water heater blanket and pipe insulation can reduce heat transfer significantly at next to no cost. Well-placed ceiling fans, especially in moist or warm climates, will help circulate and refreshen the air. These measures will save enough energy to pay for themselves easily in just a few years' time.

For homes in the Midwest and Northern states, I recommend installing blown-in or batt fiberglass up to R-38 (a measure of heat retention according to the thickness of the insulation material) in the attic space. A significant amount of heat is lost through attic spaces, and doing so also will have the least impact on the historic features of the house. However, make sure not to block the soffit (or eaves), ridge or gable vents, which provide necessary ventilation.

Insulation in the basement and sidewalls is costly and has severe ramifications for the structural stability of your home if it's not installed properly and protected

Blown-in R-38 insulation made of cellulose waste accomplishes two tasks: insulating the living space from the heat extremes of the roof and recycling newsprint.

adequately from moisture vapor and condensation. I typically don't recommend much more than a kraft-faced batt insulation at the sill plate in the basement or crawl space, with the paper facing toward the heat source to block moisture vapor.

So that's the story of the interior of your home and its systems. Any renovation project will affect many of these elements of the house, and they also are the items that most commonly need repair. Before you begin to tackle them, however, let's explore the options for using your home's interior space.

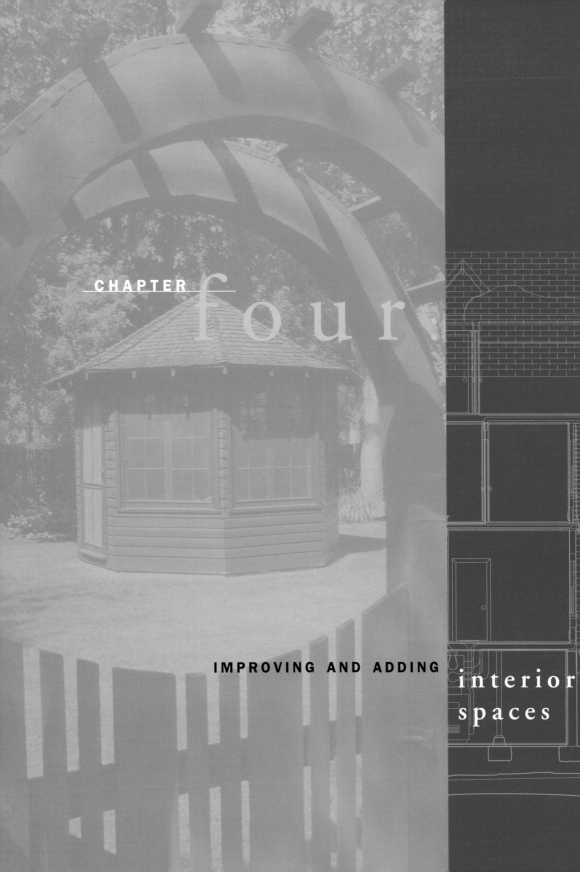

CHAPTER *four*

IMPROVING AND ADDING *interior spaces*

A few years back I read an article that compared houses of the 1920s to those of the 1990s, from the perspective of **materials and systems**, construction quality, design and overall value (can you guess where I cast my vote?). While I had my disagreements with some of the author's conclusions, I couldn't argue with one observation about modern living spaces: back in the '20s, the typical home had one and a half bathrooms and an average of four people living in the house; today, new houses have at least two and a half baths, while household numbers have shrunk to nearly the same average.

There's a certain grace that's exhibited when an addition or modification flows with and enhances the original design of a dwelling.

How does that fact affect the restoration of older houses? Clearly, the interior spaces of homes of the 1920s through the next big housing boom after World War II aren't up to most modern lifestyle needs or standards, especially when it comes to the bathrooms and the kitchen, the latter of which has become the

modern hearth. So it creates a challenge with older homes to improve the inside without ruining the historical character and form of the exterior (and the interior, for that matter).

In this chapter, we'll discuss interior improvements that add value to older homes without sacrificing their historical integrity. We'll focus on kitchens and baths, the hottest "hot buttons" for both new and restored homes, discuss storage options and fireplaces, and get beyond the main structure and talk about the value of outside structures and additions.

Interior improvements that add value Time was when the kitchen was the last place anyone wanted to be during a dinner party. Hot and stuffy, with poor ventilation and refrigeration, the kitchen wasn't even part of the main house in some designs but was instead relegated to a nearby outbuilding so its steam, heat and odors wouldn't filter into the parlor and dining area.

We've come a long way since then. Look in any home improvement magazine and you're bound to see a photo essay or two that showcases today's modern kitchen — big as a parlor, with an eat-in nook and enough appliances, counter area and cabinet space to support a small diner. Made for entertaining as much as for food preparation, today's kitchens also open onto living areas, creating flexible interior spaces.

So what if you're stuck with an outdated kitchen but don't have the budget or space to break down the walls and rebuild? You still can improve your kitchen to fit your needs while being sensitive to your home's exterior form and character, and the flow and style of its original interior design.

A kitchen renovation, from key cosmetic changes to a complete tear-out and reinstallation, is one of the most sound investments you can make, with dramatic impact on your daily life and any future sale of your house. In *Remodeling* magazine's annual "Cost vs. Value" survey, the national average for a minor, cosmetic kitchen remodel returns 94 percent on an average $8,500 investment; a complete remodel returns 90 percent of a $21,000 cost.

If you like the way your kitchen is laid out but want an updated look, your best bet is to reface your cabinets. (And, depending on the condition of your counters and floor, you also may want to swap them for newer, more durable finishes.) Such cosmetic changes, including a new paint job and better and more lighting, make a kitchen more attractive and more functional.

Cabinet refacing involves leaving the actual cabinet boxes in place and attaching strips or panels of wood veneer to their exposed surfaces (including the underside, ends and tops) to complement new cabinet doors, drawers and hardware.

Today's kitchen cabinets come in two basic styles, traditional and European, and include several options, colors and features for both.

1   European-style cabinets feature special hinges that allow the door to close flush with the cabinet face, completely hiding the hinge hardware and creating a sleeker look than is the case with traditional cabinets.

2   Traditional cabinets feature raised-panel fronts that provide a visual motif. Updating such cabinets is easy, since the front face veneer of the cabinet box easily is exchanged to match new replacement doors.

3   Raised-panel cabinet hinges pivot along the same plane as the edge of the cabinet facing, revealing the pin mechanism when the door is closed.

4   Renovation of a kitchen offers homeowners an added bonus: extra storage space, such as this over-counter dish rack, which places frequently used items in a convenient spot outside the cabinets.

5   The beauty of a Euro-style kitchen, completely renovated to adapt to the needs of busy modern lifestyles, emphasizes clean, simple lines and everyday utility.

It's really a matter of taste and consistency with the overall interior design scheme as it works with the historical character of the exterior.

Traditional cabinets often are called raised panel because the fronts feature a dimensional panel design; in addition, the hinges and hardware are exposed, and the boxes have a casing, or frame. Panel construction on cabinets and passage doors is an historic technique designed to allow the wood to expand and contract with changes in moisture and temperature; the center panel is allowed to float within the door's frame.

Traditional cabinets commonly are available in what appears to be unfinished or exposed wood, whitewashed or stained wood finishes (sometimes it's a pre-finished veneer, like oak or cherry, adhered to a less-expensive solid wood). The boxes themselves are high-grade plywood or particle board.

European, or flush-mount cabinets, are more contemporary and sleek. Their fronts are flat (or flush), and their hardware and pulls are concealed. The cabinet boxes have no casing or frame, and the units (usually in a laminate) often are available in distinctive colors and metallic finishes.

Both traditional and European-style cabinets are available through so-called stock cabinet manufacturers, as well as from local custom cabinet craftsmen. There are two primary differences: stock cabinets are built in a limited number of common sizes, while custom cabinets can be ordered to any dimensions and specific kitchen layout. Also, only the most expensive stock cabinet boxes are of

Decorating also can lean to a restored theme. Consider adding unusual fixtures and period pieces, such as the hammered, nail-decorated, tin-faced panel on this door.

sturdy plywood construction (as opposed to particle board), whereas custom cabinets almost always are — for about the same price.

Do custom cabinets last longer? It depends on how you use them. One thing's for certain, though: you have a much greater chance to get a kitchen that meets your needs if you have the cabinets designed and built from scratch.

Whether you're making cosmetic changes or restructuring your kitchen, you can make whatever cabinet space you have more efficient with a few modern storage inventions, such as rollout shelves, a lazy Susan, a bread box and integral utensil holders. You also should consider retaining the useful and eye-catching original features that fit your taste.

Retaining historic features in a traditional kitchen, such as these antique tip-out bulk storage bins, is always worthwhile. Besides being useful features, they are conversation pieces.

Refacing the cabinets and adding such elements have obvious advantages versus a complete redo: they cost less, avoid the hassle of losing the service of your kitchen for more than a few days (if that), deliver a marked aesthetic improvement and don't disturb the original floor plan or exterior elevations of the house.

Complete rehab jobs, however, afford the luxury of expanding the space to meet today's wants and needs even better. Before you start tearing out those old steel cabinets and outdated appliances, though, you'll need a plan, a budget, a schedule and, more than likely, a contractor.

Planning a new kitchen starts with asking yourself why you want to improve the space and how you intend to use it (the old "Form Follows Function" rule).

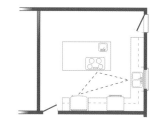

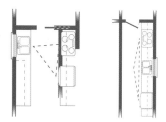

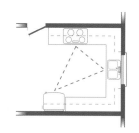

It could be that you simply have outgrown your kitchen, have inadequate storage or counter space or want more area to entertain. Maybe you're yearning for that spectacular view from a sidewall adjacent to the kitchen. You also may look at the project as an investment that will boost the value of your older home should you decide to sell it in the future. All of these reasons are valid; your job is to decide which one (or ones) apply to you.

Next, go shopping for ideas and prices, and bring along a sketch or floor plan showing your current kitchen layout and its dimensions. You should know about how much you want (or can) spend overall, what you're willing to sacrifice in terms of interior spaces and exterior finishes to get the kitchen you want and whether by moving walls you're also altering the placement of plumbing pipes, gas lines, vent stacks and electrical conduits.

Look in the phone book for nearby kitchen showrooms, which feature a variety of complete kitchens to browse; many of the home improvement centers also have similar displays, or vignettes. Both places have design services and staff to help you narrow your options and may offer contractor referrals for obtaining bids on the work (discussed in more detail in "About Your Contractor," page 152). A custom cabinet shop, by contrast, should be approached as you would a contractor — based on referrals and reputation.

As you wander the kitchen displays, take particular note of the quality of the cabinets and their true interior storage capacity. A telltale sign of good quality is

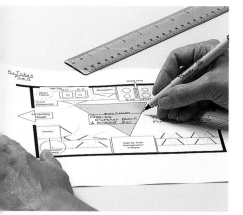

Start any kitchen renovation with a rough sketch based on careful measurements of the existing space.

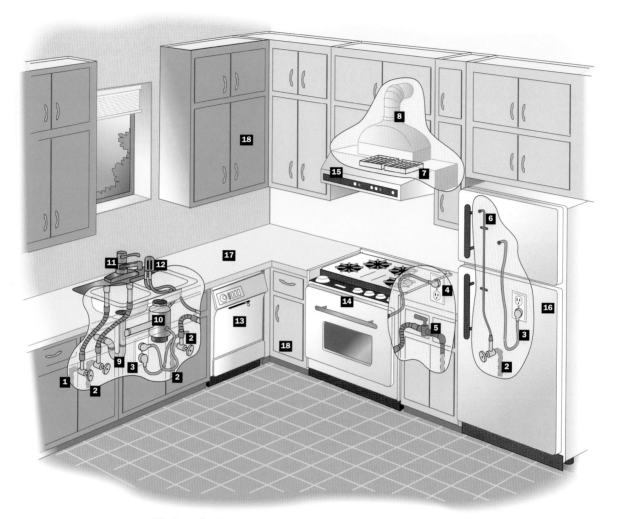

Kitchen Systems

1 Hot water supply and shut-off valve

2 Cold water supply and shutoff valve

3 110-volt AC ground-fault-protected electric outlet

4 220-volt AC grounded electric outlet

5 Natural gas supply and shutoff valve

6 Ice maker water line

7 Hood fans

8 Hood vent to outdoors

9 P trap to prevent sewer gasses from entering kitchen

10 Garbage disposal

11 Single-lever-cartridge faucet assembly

12 Dishwasher air breather

13 Dishwasher

14 Gas range combined with electric oven

15 Range hood and light

16 Refrigerator-freezer

17 Countertop

18 Cabinets

Visiting a showroom is an easy way to compare fixtures and finishing materials.

solid-wood construction of the cabinets and drawer units (instead of pressed wood behind solid-wood doors and drawers) and dovetail (or interlocking) joinery of the pieces. Another tip-off: coated steel hardware, such as the rollers and hinges, and solid hardwood doors and drawers. These features ensure durability and ease of use; they're worth the extra money.

Kitchen showrooms also will include options for lighting, faucets, countertops, flooring and appliances. Remember, though, that you're just gathering ideas and getting a sense of how your plan fits into your budget. At *most*, you want to walk out of a showroom or home center with product information, a revised floor plan of your new kitchen that includes all the elements you want and a rough idea of costs. Then, go home, gather around the dining room table and make some decisions.

As with your kitchen, redoing a bathroom can be a worthwhile investment, both for your needs and at resale. The typical 5x9-foot-bath remodel costs about $8,400, including a new tub, low-flow toilet, sink and vanity, lighting and plumbing fixtures, tile floor and tub/shower walls, and a medicine cabinet. For that kind of investment, you can expect an average return of about 77 percent. (I've got some ideas about salvaging old tubs and other products in Chapter One that will increase the payoff even more.)

Similar to a kitchen improvement project, you can make simple cosmetic changes or rip out the existing elements and start again. Many design showrooms and home centers also feature bath displays and design services because both of these projects are so popular in the home-improvement industry.

One thing most older bathrooms lack is storage, because they were designed as almost exclusively functional space. If you're confining yourself to the existing bathroom dimensions, here are some tricks to gain storage:

Depending on the interior design scheme, consider a vanity sink to replace a pedestal or wall-mounted sink for storing items that are better left unseen, such as cleaning products, paper goods and bath toys. And don't forget the walls; vertical storage, especially open shelving or wall-mounted cabinets, can provide storage for daily-use and decorative items.

A quality medicine cabinet — especially the type with modular (or movable) shelves, can accommodate your daily sundries and medicines; mirrored versions

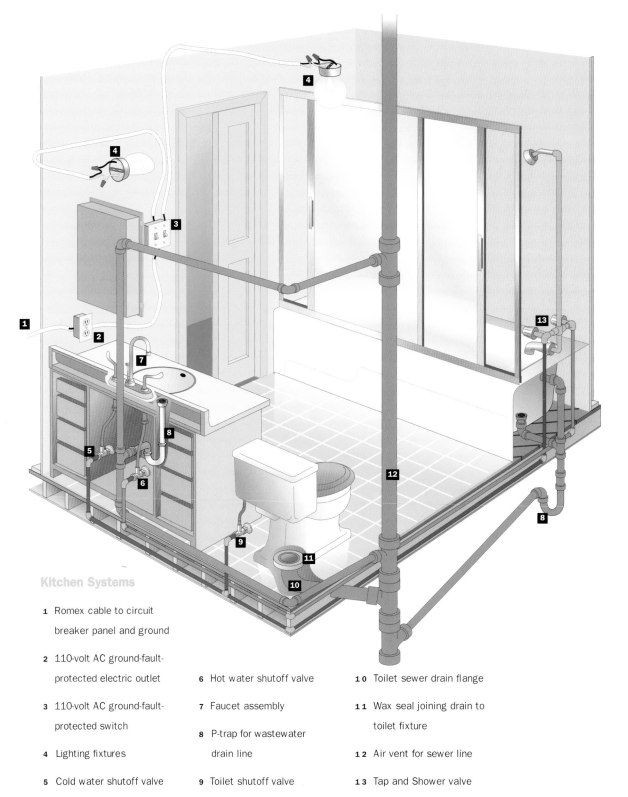

Kitchen Systems

1 Romex cable to circuit
breaker panel and ground

2 110-volt AC ground-fault-
protected electric outlet

3 110-volt AC ground-fault-
protected switch

4 Lighting fixtures

5 Cold water shutoff valve

6 Hot water shutoff valve

7 Faucet assembly

8 P-trap for wastewater
drain line

9 Toilet shutoff valve

10 Toilet sewer drain flange

11 Wax seal joining drain to
toilet fixture

12 Air vent for sewer line

13 Tap and Shower valve

Whether your bathroom upgrade is a simple refacing of cabinets or a complete tear-out, keep your storage needs in mind at each stage of the renovation.

"Whatever your plans for new plumbing fixtures, fittings and storage, try your best to put them in about the same place."

— BOB YAPP

are not only functional but help make a small space appear larger. And, in the tub or shower, waterproof wall-mounted or hanging units store shampoos and soaps. You also might want to include a nifty, multitowel rack that attaches to the back of the door.

Many of the bathrooms I've rehabilitated feature other storage options, especially when the preference is for a pedestal sink. I've put in antique tables and wardrobes in place of vanity sinks and wall cabinets. These aren't valuable heirlooms; rather, they are items that combine storage with a sense of historically appropriate style.

As with a complete kitchen redo, moving walls (and thus the various utilities) likely will require new or upgraded electrical, plumbing and other mechanical systems, adding time and cost to the project. Therefore, whatever you do with new plumbing fixtures, outlets and lighting, try your best to put the new stuff in approximately the same place.

Beyond kitchens and baths   While perhaps the most dramatic, kitchens and baths aren't the only areas that can improve and boost the value of your interior spaces. There are several common-sense and inexpensive ways to make even an older home more comfortable.

The simplest is to repair and paint the interior walls. Patching, filling cracks and painting, especially with a bright, neutral color (like white), not only looks clean but will perk up any interior and make it appear more spacious. (Chapter Three covers more extensive interior surface problems and fixes.)

Washing windows — both inside and out — makes an impression that far exceeds the effort required.

Cleaning   A few other effective and relatively inexpensive projects can make your home more livable. The first is to spring for a complete and professional carpet cleaning once a year. You'll be surprised (and likely a little alarmed) at the dirt, grime, dust, stains and other unhealthy particles that can collect on your carpets in just a year's time. For about $40 per 100 square feet, professional carpet cleaners will remove stains and refreshen the carpeted areas of your home, providing a cleaner-looking, more comfortable and healthier indoor environment for you and your family. Oriental rugs should be sent to a rug-cleaning specialist to protect their investment value.

Finally, though we all hate to do it, cleaning your windows makes a huge difference. Clean windows bring in light, which can help warm a cool area of the house or provide a comfortable reading area. And all it takes is a bucket of warm, soapy water, a squeegee and a rag on the inside and first-floor windows. If you don't want to climb a ladder, a hose with a good spray nozzle will remove the dirt and grime from those upper-story windows well enough. Some replacement windows make that job even easier; by design, they tilt inward, allowing you to clean both sides of the window-pane from the inside. [See Chapter Three for details about replacement windows.]

For the cost of a few gallons of good-quality latex flat and a slightly contrasting semigloss for the trim work, you can give your interior a real face-lift.

The single thing that really can make a house look terrible is clutter (and, yes, I'm a classic offender myself). With more people working at home and more two-income households, I certainly empathize with the lack of time to do more than stack stuff around the house. But clutter is not only unsightly, it actually makes your rooms and yard areas appear smaller.

Older homes are notorious for their lack of storage space. Sure, they may have attics and basements, but they usually are inaccessible, inconvenient or unreliable (like a wet basement) for today's storage needs.

If you can't claim the attic or basement for storage, consider shelving compartments in the laundry, closets and pantry, with stackable bins and wall-mounted shelves. You also can take a lesson from your ancestors and use furniture for storing such items as CDs and computer equipment. Bottom line: getting clutter off the floor and onto a vertical plane goes a remarkably long way; you'll be amazed how much bigger your house feels.

Of course, one main area of clutter is the laundry. In older homes, the laundry area usually is stuffed down in the dark, damp basement. It's totally illogical when you think about where the dirty clothes are generated — upstairs in the bed-rooms — which means you have to haul them down to the basement. It's like putting a kitchen in the attic.

There are two ways to solve this problem. The first is to find a space upstairs to build out into a laundry room. Many pre-1930s homes have maid's quarters or other small bedrooms that are ideal for master bath additions or laundry room redos. These areas also may be large enough to gain closet space for adjacent rooms in addition to a laundry. With this option, however, you'll have to bring water (and maybe gas) lines, heavy-duty electrical wiring and a direct ventilation system to the space.

If all this is too costly or impractical, go the less-expensive way with a laundry chute to the basement by reclaiming an abandoned mechanical chase. The time and effort will be worth it.

About fireplaces   Despite the modern phenomena of the kitchen as a gathering place and the television as the focal point of the family room, the traditional hearth, or fireplace, still warms the heart more than anything else. In fact, most new homes today have two, with the second hearth in such places as

Use the repair and renovation of an existing fireplace to add additional warmth to a room through built-ins, such as these bookcases that adjoin the hearth.

the master bedroom or bathroom, the kitchen or the den. There's just something about the flicker of flames and the warmth generated by a fire.

For historic reasons, I first recommend trying to restore an existing masonry fireplace and its chimney bricks or concrete blocks using a professional mason. Occasionally, I'll find a chimney whose original firebox has been bricked over or covered by plaster or drywall, or one that served a freestanding wood stove or heater that since has been removed. In these cases, space limitations and historical preferences call for a site-built masonry fireplace, where the size of the box can be dictated and an existing ventilation system utilized without disturbing historical features.

If you plan to use an existing chimney, make sure the flue is relined and of the correct size; a minimum 8-inch clearance in the finished flue is a good rule, depending on the size of the firebox. The chimney should be inspected for cracks or voids in the masonry or mortar joints and should extend 3 feet above the highest point of the roof. Voids in the flue liner or chimney can result in a buildup of soot, which will limit proper ventilation of smoke and toxic combustion gasses, allowing them to flow back into the room. You also will need a spark arrester attached to the top of the flue to inhibit airborne sparks from landing on the roofing material.

Of course, a wood-burning masonry fireplace is optimum if you're eager to preserve the past. But given regulations against wood burning in some areas, gas

Many times, salvaged fireplace mantels and decorative facings may be recycled to complete a fireplace within its period and style.

logs may provide a more energy-efficient, environmentally sound choice. Make sure you check with your local government regulatory offices, masons or fireplace suppliers before you begin construction.

In situations where there is no existing chimney or where building a masonry fireplace and flue would be impractical, too costly or detrimental to a home's historic character, I recommend premanufactured fireplace units. Some of these metal boxes feature direct venting systems, allowing you to ventilate smoke and gasses out a sidewall instead of through a chimney. Prefabs also require less installation time than masonry fireboxes and are available with both wood-burning and natural-gas options.

Outside structures and additions Homes built before the turn of the century have two distinct differences from modern homes when it comes to land. First, homesteads simply had more if it. Second, they required outbuildings that were in close proximity, but not attached to, the main house for garaging horse-drawn carriages and storing farm equipment.

Today, these estates are treasured and often protected historically. Yet attention to the restoration and maintenance of the main house may have neglected the outbuildings. But these structures not only have historical significance, they can be recycled and reused as living space, automobile garages or storage areas. Carriage houses and barns are typical adaptive reuse projects; restoring them should be approached with the same care and respect given to the main house.

An added garage (top) retains the characteristics of this Victorian-era house, while a former carriage house (bottom) provides a valued extra room.

125

One obvious place to look for more space is an unfinished attic. It might be just right for a hobby room or to allow your teenager to spread out.

Additions Conceptually, I don't have a problem with adding rooms to an older home, even if they change the exterior elevation. They can add value, modernize the interior to meet today's standards and needs, trigger the often necessary upgrades of mechanical and energy systems and even enhance the exterior appearance of an older home. In reality, however, I've seen too many scab-ons ruin the historic, meticulously designed character of a home for the sake of a playroom, where mass and scale, roof forms and exterior materials, are at best an afterthought.

A tasteful, appropriately scaled addition or new, detached building on the site considers these factors in concert with the intended use of the new space. At the same time, additions also must be distinctive enough from the main building form to not mask the history of the original structure. In terms of historic preservation practices and guidelines, additions are acceptable if they maintain this balance; in fact, most older homes have evolved throughout their history to accommodate changes in lifestyle and technology, often with additions to the original structure. The guidelines outlined in Chapter One recognize the historical significance of well-executed additions. Who's to say that yours can't have equal integrity and value?

To meet the expectations of the historic preservation guidelines, make your addition to the back or sides of the house. This will depend on where you have available land (within allowed setbacks) and the design of the new interior room. Only in situations where land on your property is scarce do I recommend adding an upstairs or second floor

Other than the ease— and price — of its construction, it is difficult to understand what logic produced this inappropriate addition.

(unless you're adding to an existing second story) or adding the bulk of the new space to the front. Rarely, if ever, do I see an addition or major alteration to the front elevation that does not compromise its historic character and value. You also may want to consider a detached building or adding to the top of a detached garage to gain the new space you need.

In any case, make sure the add-on is to scale, follows existing roof forms and window heights and styles, and uses the same exterior materials and applications as the original house.

One of the best resources I've found on the subject of additions to older homes is the book *Architectural Plans for Adding On or Remodeling* by architect Jerold Axelrod. A student of residential design forms, the author provides hundreds of helpful sketches

illustrating various kinds of additions for several types of homes, roof forms and exterior elevations. One of them is sure to come close to your home's design. My favorite chapter, though, deals with what not to do.

Also, the Secretary of the Interior's Preservation Brief #14, which you can obtain at no cost from your state or local preservation office, specifically addresses concerns regarding exterior additions to historic buildings. In it, you'll learn that "freezing a building in time" is not the expected goal of preservation, nor is getting the property listed on the National Register; rather, this 12-page brief helps you recognize the changes that are significant and worth preserving, those that are not and how to ensure that a new addition will add to the home's comfort, space, value and character. Check it out.

If no outbuildings exist, but you need more storage space, I often recommend a tasteful yard shed to hold everything from the snow blower, rakes and shovels to the barbecue kettle, pet food, garden tools and sporting equipment. This option is much better than cluttering up the garage and, done right, makes a valuable addition to your own "estate."

Let's quickly dismiss with what not to do, which is to buy a cheesy shed kit from your local lumberyard. They usually are too small and will never match the style, color and basic architectural character of your house; in short, they'll stick out like a sore thumb. Besides, they often are built cheaply, with "structural" elements that float on walls, capable of supporting nothing. I urge you to stretch your pocketbook a little and have one site built by a contractor.

One of the best site-built sheds I ever saw was in a home improvement magazine. It was designed to be integral to the corner of a perimeter fence, thus achieving a subtle place in the yard. It was big enough to hold a rider mower (including a short ramp to the door), as well as the various items just mentioned. It was sturdy, built as a shed should be, on a foundation with properly structured systems of walls and roof. Building it into the fence was ingenious, eliminating the expense of two walls.

A site-built shed, like any other structural addition (attached or not), may require a building permit before you begin construction. Permits are designed to regulate health and safety in buildings as well as to watchdog such zoning issues as setbacks, building height and use. While it is unlikely your shed will have

This custom-built gazebo completes the yard and offers both a shelter for outdoor dining and a focus for other garden activities. Its rustic style perfectly matches a Craftsman-style bungalow.

Gazebos Gazebos, or freestanding outdoor structures, were an important part of early American architecture; like decks, patios and fences (discussed in Chapter Five), they performed a function in the overall landscape scheme. Early gazebos provided accessibility to the outdoors with protection against the elements.

Before you build a gazebo, consider what its modern function will be— an intimate gathering place, a shelter from a sudden downpour or perhaps home to a hot tub. A gazebo's function not only will determine its shape and size but its proximity to the main house. Its form and the materials used to build and finish it will depend on that function as well as on the design and style of your house.

Like a deck, a gazebo is a structure; as a freestanding unit, it may require you to obtain a permit for its construction. You'll also want to call the various utility companies to check for underground lines before you start to excavate for its foundation.

Similar to the specifications for a deck, your gazebo will need a solid footing for its frame and recommended finishes for its materials. Because the finished product should resemble your restored house in style and character, it also should pick up one of its details, such as fish-scale shingles or a metal roof.

Unlike prefabricated yard sheds, gazebo kits available via mail order or from a local supplier are generally of good quality; the problem is that you often are limited to a number of designs and types of structures and finishes that may not match its intended purpose or the design of your house. In that case, I'd suggest hiring a contractor to build a gazebo on site; it will cost you more (by perhaps 20 percent) than a kit, but you'll ensure that you electrical or plumbing, which will add cost and require more permits, its structure and placement likely will have to be checked by a local building official to make sure it complies with local building and zoning codes. You also will want to call the local utility companies to have them spot underground lines and pipes so you know where to avoid potential problems.

If you risk it and build without taking these measures, you open yourself up to fines and may have a hard time at resale, when title companies and banks check all property before approving the transfer of ownership.

CHAPTER *five:*

YARD AND LANDSCAPE improvements

A well-planned and carefully tended yard
is an essential element of the character
and even the **historical value** of a
restored home. As we discussed in Chapter Two, architects and builders of the late 1800s and
early part of this century thought about homes from the outside in. That philosophy included the home's relationship to its natural surroundings, as well as
how the folks inside enjoyed views or gained access to the outside areas through
patio doors, balconies and pathways to outdoor structures.

Much of a restoration or
renovation project concerns
the home itself. Taking the
same care with all of the
surrounding yard and landscape will finish the project
and act as a showcase for the
home's architecture.

While existing trees and natural vegetation often helped determine how a
home was sited (or oriented) on a given property, the home's design and details
dictated the formal layout and plantings of yard and garden. Like the materials
to build the home, many of the trees, shrubs and flowers were native to the
area, creating a cohesiveness that reinforced the appeal, comfort and historic
character of the home.

Landscaping isn't just shrubs and trees but rock walls and water features, grassy
berms and gravel pathways, concrete patios and wood decks. In this chapter,

we'll touch on these elements, provide insight into planning a yard that is appropriate to your home's style and character, and offer tips about building, repairing and maintaining these landscape features.

About your landscaping Planning and maintaining a yard can get lost in the hustle and bustle of a home renovation project. But it is as important as any work done on the house and should be figured into the overall budget and schedule. Simply, quality landscaping enhances the value of the restoration work done on the home's exterior finishes and details, and leads visitors (and you) to notice particular features and points of entry that mark the character and appeal of the home and surrounding property.

There are some simple ways to create and maintain a good-looking yard without breaking the bank. A patch of lawn is a relatively low-cost feature, especially if you select the appropriate turf for your geographic area and climate. The same goes for plantings that are native to the area and naturally fill in the landscape plan without extra effort or maintenance [for more about this subject, see "Xeriscaping," on page 140].

The key to keeping costs low is to determine a budget and work with a landscape designer or nursery to plan your yard before you plant anything. These folks will know which plants and ground covers will best meet your needs. In addition, proper and periodic maintenance (discussed further in this chapter) is vital to keeping your yard dollars in check.

Yard and Landscape

1 House

2 Garage

3 Asphalt Driveway

4 Sidewalks

5 Street

6 Lawn

7 Porch

8 Deck

9 Brick patio, pond and watercourse

10 Stepstone path

11 Vegetable garden

12 Decorative flower border

13 Natural stone paving and garden bench

Planning If you want to improve or reclaim your yard as part of an overall restoration project, I have one major piece of advice: take a hike — that is, around the neighborhood or historic districts of your town. While there literally are thousands of books on gardening and outdoor projects, including a significant number about historical landscapes, the best place to get information is in your own "backyard." That way, you'll understand and appreciate the regional and local influences on the area surrounding your home.

As you walk, you'll discover there's a reason you like the yards around some homes and not others, even if all are relatively well-maintained. I'm betting the yards you like are those that truly flow with the architecture of the home. A landscape architect I know easily explains this by categorizing homes and their yards into two kinds: symmetrical (or formal) and asymmetrical (or informal).

Look at your front door, then at the right and left sides of the front elevation. Are they mirror images, like you'd find on a Federal- or Georgian-style house? Such architectural formality should be carried into the yard to reinforce the design of your home.

The primary element of a formal garden design is a central pathway that leads from the curb to the front door. Like the facade of a symmetrically designed house, the plantings on either side of the path (as well as on crossing or secondary paths) should mirror one another. Flower beds, shrubs, dwarf trees or a combination of these and other plantings can vary in color and kind, but not in height. Secondary paths, hedges and fences running parallel and perpendicular to the central

About your lawn Well-maintained lawns usually are the canvases for any landscape plan. They also add value to your home, boosting it by perhaps 5 to 7 percent, according to those in the know. But as simple as they may look to maintain (just mow it, right?), lawns and their care may be the most misunderstood of all yard work.

The biggest problem I see is overcutting, or scalping. To maintain a healthy, active lawn, you should avoid cutting more than a third of the height of the grass at any one time; any more will stunt and shock the turf, inhibiting its growth

and causing yellow patches. It also is important to know what type of grass you have and when it grows best. For instance, fescue flourishes in the fall and spring, while Bermuda grass is dormant in the fall. Knowing this information will direct how often you should mow during peak growth times to help maintain healthy lawns.

Aerating is the best thing you can do for your lawn, more so even than irrigation or fertilization. Poking holes in the lawn's compacted soil allows water to penetrate to the roots, for better growth. Combined with weed control (which eliminates competition for water and nutrients) and leaf removal (to prevent smothering and kiling grass), aerating will provide fast results at a minimum cost.

Irrigation is a touchy subject given concerns about water use, but it is essential to a healthy lawn. The key is knowing when and how much to water; I

recommend a deep watering in the early morning, perhaps up to 1 inch every other day during the summer months.

To test the precipitation of your irrigation (by either manual sprinklers or an automatic system), place an empty coffee can in the center of your lawn and note the amount of time required to collect 1 inch of water in the can.

Finally, let's say that you purchase an older home with a lawn that needs some attention, perhaps to the point of replacing major sections of turf. If there are just a few bare spots, try aerating and overseeding to bolster them; if the lawn is dead, you may have to invest in a complete tilling (or disking) to about 3 to 6 inches in depth, excavation and leveling of the site, adding fertilizer and other nutrients, and resodding or seeding. It can cost up to a few thousand dollars to hire a professional to renovate a dead lawn.

path define the boundaries of the property and should be uniform, as well. Typically, the site itself is flat, either by nature, design or excavation.

Another feature particular to formal gardens is the art object — a fountain, statue, iron urn or sundial — at the end of each long, straight pathway and at the termini of the property's boundaries. Any outbuildings in a formal yard also should be consistent with the design of the house, including its symmetry and use of traditional materials and finishes.

As home styles became less formal and more fluid, landscape design followed. Bungalows of the Arts & Crafts era, for instance, feature steep roofs with odd angles, wraparound porches and bump-outs. Their rambling, natural design should be carried through in the landscape.

Asymmetrical homes are best-served by yards with winding paths and creeks, and a wild mix of plants and shrubs and trees whose branches are allowed to grow into naturally sculpted canopies. While a path may end at the front door, it should take its time, leading guests through the garden and encouraging them to interact with it as they would in the wilderness.

Similarly, outbuildings in an informal yard should be rustic, as if built simply and only from the surrounding resources of tree twigs, stumps and rocks. They should be randomly sited rather than placed at the end of a path. Unlike with formal garden design, the natural contours of the land dictate the plan.

"While a path may end at the front door, it should take its time, leading guests through the garden and encouraging them to interact with it as they would in the wilderness."

— BOB YAPP

About Xeriscaping **The term "xeriscaping" was coined in 1981 and is defined as the practice of water conservation through creative landscaping. Xeriscaping was developed to help reduce the amount of water needed for landscaping, which is typically 50 percent of a home's water usage. The concept goes hand in hand with other low-maintenance or natural landscaping, such as meadow or cactus gardens.**

A xeriscape garden can reduce outside water use by as much as 80 percent without sacrificing the design or any historically based objectives. In fact, xeriscape fits perfectly with the goal of maintaining or restoring an historic landscape or garden because it encourages the use of local and regional plantings that have adapted to the region's climate and rely on seasonal and annual rainfall as their primary or sole source of water.

Of course, there are hybrids. American architecture is a melting pot of heritages and designs combined to create unique forms. One result can be an overall informality with perhaps an element of symmetry along one facade, such as the entry or rear of the house.

Similarly, the landscape can respect both forms, typically with a formal court-yard directly in front of a symmetrical feature on an otherwise informal house, surrounded by less formally designed plantings outside of the courtyard. Another hybrid: asymmetrical plantings within a formal landscape grid, which was common in late-nineteenth-century Colonial design.

Whatever the style, remember that original landscape elements, such as stone or brick walls, paved walkways or stepping-stones, fences, wells, gazebos and arbors are valuable to the historical character of the property and ought to be maintained and restored, if only for their form rather than function.

However, maintaining an historic garden does not require you to keep every overgrown shrub and tree on the property. No garden can be maintained properly or kept healthy if the trees and plants compete with each other for water, sunlight and space. Overgrown foliage can be potentially hazardous or create maintenance problems, such as tree branches that hang over a power line or roof section, or plantings that block views or limit sunlight from drying out cedar shingles after a rainstorm.

No matter what kind of yard you have, proper care is essential to maintaining its value and lessening its impact on the environment in terms of water usage, production of yard waste and pest control.

A carefully planned landscape integrates the outdoor and indoor living areas of the home, adding to its enjoyment and utility.

Basic maintenance can be boiled down to five steps, or tasks: weeding, feeding, pruning, pest control and watering. By far the most important of these tasks is watering, because proper irrigation helps minimize the need for the other chores.

For example, overwatering is a lightning rod for pests, which are attracted to standing water and thrive in moist, warm areas. To keep them under control, know the right amount of water each plant needs (or plan a garden in which the plants require similar amounts of water), and perhaps add a water feature, such as a pond or birdbath, to attract birds and other wildlife that feed on many garden pests.

If you hate to prune, plan for dwarf trees and other slow-growing varieties that, even if left to assume their natural shapes, don't create an overgrowth problem. And consider reducing the "green apron" in front of and around your house with paved areas, plantings or a ground cover; not only will you reduce water usage significantly, you won't have as much to mow.

Proper irrigation depends on two factors: the condition of the soil and the plants you select. It's fairly easy to find out the type or types of soil in your area from a local nursery, then make improvements to its condition so that your plants can thrive. If you want to use an automatic irrigation system, make sure to check the sensors and outlets periodically; a blocked or poorly regulated water flow hinders your ability to manage water as the basis of your maintenance program.

To remain true to the history of your home and garden, take care to select plants and other landscape features that are indigenous to your area; it keeps water use to a minimum because the plants and flowers already have adapted to the local climate.

Outside underfoot   Since the advent of poured concrete in the 1930s, paved areas such as paths, patios and driveways have become common features of American landscape design. To minimize their impact on the natural surroundings, plan for them sparingly; figure out the natural traffic patterns around your house to limit trampling of shrubs and flowers. In addition, you'll want to understand how a paved area will be used for walking, hauling materials or for vehicles, and select materials and construction methods that will support such use over time.

Like concrete used in the construction of a foundation [see Chapter Two], so-called hardscapes are subject to deterioration and damage from water infiltration and use; over time, if not properly sloped or shielded from water runoff or collection, paved areas will crack as the soil underneath them compacts and settles.

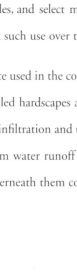

1 Brick paving laid in a basket-weave pattern.

2 While relatively easy to install, an asphalt driveway requires regular sealing to retain its beauty and prevent water from penetrating cracks in the surface.

3 A herringbone brick pattern.

4 Brick-on-sand walks, laid with extra spacing between each of the pavers, will weather in over time. Some homeowners prefer the ease of maintenance of tightly spaced bricks, which prevents the growth of turf between the courses.

5 Bricks laid in a half-basket-weave pattern.

6 Choosing attractive paving for walks and driveways helps complete the exterior of the home.

If you need to repair or replace an existing paved area, first determine the source of the water or abuse and correct it. You simply may have to add an extender and splash block to a nearby downspout, fix or replace a gutter above the driveway, turn the spray of your lawn sprinklers away from a path or find another route for your rider mower, garbage cans or wheelbarrow.

Depending on its condition, a patio, path or driveway may be repaired in several ways, from cleaning and sealing minor cracks with a flexible masonry caulk to actually lifting back a section to its original elevation. What you don't want to do is hide the problem; as with your home's siding and roofing, I discourage any technique that covers the original material, which likely will compound the problem and affect the historic character of the property. In addition, methods for capping an existing concrete slab can be expensive and difficult to apply properly.

If a section of concrete has sunk below another, an effective way to fix the problem is a technique called mud jacking (or slab jacking). Simply, a contractor will drill holes into the section near the crack or separation and pump a concrete slurry underneath the slab. The pressure pushes the section pack into place, and the holes are patched over. Again, if you've solved the cause of the problem, mud jacking likely will keep your path or driveway flat. And mud jacking typically is about two-thirds the cost of a complete replacement.

If you have to replace a paved area, take steps to ensure the problem doesn't recur. Once the concrete has been stripped away, make sure the ground underneath is prepared properly, which includes grading the surface to a slight

crown to direct rain and runoff away from the finish area. The concrete itself should be about 6 inches thick, and a wire mesh should be installed within the concrete slab during the pour to provide reinforcement and limit cracking. Finally, filling control joints with an expansive (usually asphalt) sealer will allow sections of the surface area to expand and contract with changes in climate.

If paving or repaving seems too daunting or is too expensive, there's always gravel, paving stones and stepping-stones, which require less-intensive preparation. Because they are not permanent features, they also intrude less on the natural environment. In addition, individual stones can be replaced if they break, and the direction or design can be altered much more easily than can a paved walkway.

What's great about all of today's hardscape options is the variety of shapes and colors from which to choose. A trip to the lumberyard or local home center reveals interlocking sections of granite, sandstone and concrete, not to mention the traditional rectangular red brick. You can even purchase aged brick to help match sections of old, historic paths or walkways that are being replaced.

The combination of lanterns, lighted paths, birch trees and benches makes for pleasant evenings (top). An extra touch of texture, shown here in a slate walk, creates visual interest (bottom).

As with a poured concrete or asphalt material, pavers require a stable base, good drainage and proper maintenance to keep their shape and function. I never recommend that pavers be mortared in place because of the amount of expansion and contraction they experience in various climates; rather, they should be dry set with a fine sand tamped between the cracks. They can be arranged in various patterns to lead folks to a focal point, surround and separate an herb, flower or vegetable garden, or create a gathering area.

Exterior Construction   As part of the overall character of the property, decks and fences need to be respectful of their surroundings. But more so than paths and plants, these elements have several important jobs to do, so their design is based first on their function.

With a deck or fence, first ask yourself why you want it and how it will be used. A well-planned deck can be for everything from entertaining to simply extending the indoor living spaces to the outdoors. With fences, your reasons may range from keeping pets and children corralled (and protected) in the yard to gaining more privacy to preserving an historic feature. Once you've determined the main function for your deck or fence, appropriate material choices, design and finishes will follow logically.

Decks   A deck typically requires a professional and a building permit to provide assurances for proper construction and compliance with health and safety standards required by the building codes in your area. A deck is a structure, so take time to research the type and style you want, what it will contain (such as seating, planters, furniture or even a hot tub) and what materials are appropriate for its use and complementary to your home's style.

Your best starting place is deck design and building books available at your local nursery or home center. Then walk around the neighborhood to see what others have done, noting what you like and don't like. The biggest mistake you can make with a deck is to "wing it," because you'll end up trying to alter the design to accommodate a missing feature.

A deck's structure starts with support posts, the number and size of these members dependent on the size and scale of the deck, its height off the ground and the amount of weight it will be expected to support. Any structural member that touches the ground should be either redwood (which naturally resists rot and decay) or pressure-treated lumber, my personal preference.

As a structure, a deck needs to be supported properly with a solid foundation. There are several ways to accomplish this, but I prefer deep, wide footings about 9 inches below the frost line, reinforced with steel bars (or rebar) installed vertically to grade level. Once the concrete in the footing is cured (or dry), a sonnet (or thick cardboard) tube is installed to extend a few inches above grade and enclose the rebar from the footing; concrete then is poured to the top of the tube, and the area around the tube is filled with compacted dirt. A metal anchor holds the structural post in place on the footing. This method keeps the wood post from touching the ground, which can cause it to rot; if the post eventually does rot, there is still a structural footing upon which to rebuild the deck.

Local interpretations of building codes and regionally accepted practices may prevail in other areas of the country, but I suggest "overbuilding" a deck no matter where you live to make sure it is a secure, safe and long-lasting structure.

The floor structure and finishes, including the railing system and deck boards, can be any wood material you choose; cedar, pressure-treated fir and redwood are common, durable materials. And there's no law that says you have to lay the

Decks and fences help define the yard and its use. While they are functional elements of the landscaping, they also provide the opportunity to add interest and beauty.

deck boards perfectly straight. I've seen decks with intricate patterns, such as herringbone, which give the area a distinctive appearance. But there are laws regarding the height of the railing and the space between the spindles, both of which are regulated by building codes. In my area, railings must be at least 36 inches above the deck and spindles spaced no wider than 4 inches apart; make sure you know what the regulations are in your town.

As your deck nears completion, you may notice that your builder has butted the deck boards together rather than leaving a gap for expansion. This practice undoubtedly means that the lumber had a higher moisture content and is expected to shrink over time; pressure-treated lumber, I've found, often falls into this category. If the deck boards are dry, you will need to leave gaps for expansion; holding a decking nail between two boards during hammering will create a consistent $\frac{1}{16}$-inch gap throughout the area.

Finally, a word about preservative treatments and sealers: I've never been convinced that they do a lick of good on a deck; besides, you're paying for wood that has natural decay- and rot-resistant qualities and therefore shouldn't require a protective coating. These compounds also require regular maintenance and reapplication, and they don't inhibit wood's natural aging unless they contain chemicals to block ultraviolet radiation. Even then, the wood will age and fade to a gray tone. Best, then, to just let it do so naturally.

Fences   Fence building follows a similar process to deck building, requiring you to first think about what function you want the fence to perform and choosing a design and materials that complement your home's style. Depending on the intended use of the fence, your design also can allow for ventilation, incorporate decorative details and cut-outs or be constructed in a woven pattern.

Unlike yard sheds, fences purchased from a lumberyard tend to be an easy, high-quality and comparably priced alternative to building one from scratch, especially if you have designs on an intricate-weave or ventilated fence that might require a professional. Usually available in 8-foot sections, premade fence bays come in a wide variety of styles, heights and materials, and are offered with such accessories as gates and arbors.

Safety and Security

1 Landscape and walkway safety lighting

2 Under-step lighting and non-slip treads

3 General area lighting

4 Intrusion sensor tape within window glass

5 Closed circuit TV system

6 Alarm for intruder and fire alert

appendices

about your contractor

Throughout this book, as well as on television, radio and in my newsletter, I've tried to stress that any renovation or restoration work on an older home is **a process** that requires proper planning and investigation beforehand. The same is especially true when it comes time to find and hire a good contractor.

For the moment, let's assume you've decided to hire out the work rather than attempt to do it yourself, an alternative discussed later in this appendix. Making this choice, however, does not eliminate you from having a significant role in the work that will be done on your house; it merely redefines it.

One of the first things I ask people who are considering an historic renovation is what they're willing to commit to the project in terms of time and money. By hiring a contractor, you won't need to manage the actual construction, which is a virtually full-time task. However, you must make time for project administration and planning.

Choosing a contractor to implement your renovation plans is the most important step in the whole process.

Because only you can determine and control the overall expectations, budget, deadlines, contract terms and hiring practices, how well you perform your role as project administrator will be the key to your project's success. A lot of folks can install cabinets, refinish floors and rebuild plaster cornices, but no one else knows exactly what you want and expect from the work that will be done on your house.

Planning Like the construction phase itself, planning a home restoration is a step-by-step process, requiring a dedicated schedule and measurable, achievable goals; like a puzzle, all the pieces must be there for it to fall properly into place.

The basic steps are: assessing your needs (from your own inspection as well as a formal, detailed list from a home inspector; see Chapter One), scouting for ideas, gathering referrals, finding design professionals (if necessary), determining budgets and obtaining financing. It's also important to attach deadlines to complete each step, making sure they are realistic, given family and job commitments as well as upcoming business trips, vacations and holidays. And once you've set the deadlines, stick to them (it'll be good practice for when the construction work begins).

If this process sounds a bit daunting, it is — especially for a major renovation project. While the more detailed information you provide a contractor, the better, few folks are well-versed in the lingo, much less the construction process.

In almost all instances I recommend homeowners hire an independent restoration or renovation consultant to provide a scope of the work and supply blueprints and specifications for bid estimates or contract negotiations. Such independent consultants offer an unbiased view; their expertise lies in assessing the extent of a project and offering advice about priorities, budget and schedule specific to the restoration work — skills that may vary in degree and quality among inspectors, general contractors and architects. I've also known these consultants to be hired to manage the project for the owner. To find one, stop by your state or local historic preservation office for a list of consultants and architects who specialize in restoration work.

With without a consultant, a preliminary needs assessment will start the process of refining the scope of the project and building a list of products needed for it. From that, you can determine what absolutely has to be done and also what you'd like to have done, depending on your budget, the historical impact on your home and your lifestyle needs.

Next, do some scouting. As we discussed in Chapter Four with reference to kitchen and bath rehabs, visit showrooms and home centers, take notice of the restoration work your friends and family have had done, tour houses in historic neighborhoods and even the models of new home developments, and attend local, home-related expositions and shows. And take notes — build a library, or at least a file, of ideas.

As you tour homes where the work is similar to the project you're considering, ask about the contractor; friends, family and neighbors are the absolute best sources for referrals (in addition to the state preservation office). Inquire about work habits, the overall condition of the job site, cleanup practices and materials storage. Jot down the names of any recommended contractors; we'll discuss how to narrow that list later.

Finally, determine how you plan to finance the project, specifically what amount you can garner and afford from loans and savings, which will, in turn, dictate your budget for the project and the scope of the work. And, be prepared to share it with your contractor.

I know, conventional wisdom (and your father-in-law) says to keep what you're willing to spend close to the vest.

But, in fact, sharing this information protects everyone, allowing you and the other professionals you may be using — such as a consultant or architect, kitchen designer or interior decorator — to develop a realistic plan for the work. Being up front with the budget eliminates the disappointment of having to downscale a project, sometimes even midway through the work, or having to swap a desired product or material for one of lesser quality and cost.

Once you've completed these steps it's time to start refining the scope of construction and planning for any necessary design work that will further define the project or projects. Depending on the nature or intricacy (a single room, elevation alteration or whole-house renovation), design services range from a draftsperson to a renovation consultant to a full-service architect, all with various skill levels and costs.

Some building contractors offer a design-build scenario, in which both design and construction services are available under one roof. Such companies frequently offer discounts on the design if you contract with them for both, but I'm wary of their motives. It seems to me that there's an inherent, direct conflict of interest when a contractor is hired both to provide the specifications and help set the budget. Instead, base your choices on folks who have a successful track record with historic renovation and restoration work, and separate the design and build contracts.

With designs and preliminary specifications in hand, the time has come to narrow your list of contractors. But before you contact any, call the state contractor licensing agency to check them out. Licensing not only indicates commitment and a competent level of skill and knowledge, it assures adequate insurance coverage. In addition, it may be difficult, if not impossible, for an unlicensed contractor to pull permits for the work, which will cause delays and possibly incur financial penalties.

Next, check with such local industry watchdog agencies as the Consumer Protection Agency, the Better Business Bureau and the state Attorney General's office. Don't be surprised to find a few contractors on your list on file with these agencies; home improvement complaints are common, if not always justified. Conversely, in the case of the Better Business Bureau, contractors are only listed if a claim against them has been settled; those pending are not on record.

Finally, look carefully through the marketing materials provided by each contractor on your list and check out their ads in the local paper or other publications. Buzzwords such as "specializing in home renovations" or "historic preservation work" are key, but also be on the lookout for references to professional organizations and mentions of warranties, all signs of a good contractor candidate. The goal is to narrow your choices to those contractors who are experienced and especially skilled in home and historic renovations.

This preliminary weeding-out process should narrow your list considerably, perhaps to three or four names. At this point, you need to make a choice between the traditional, three-bid process or negotiating with just one contractor.

The three-bid rule goes like this: you solicit cost estimates on your scope of work (including design drawings and specifications) from three contractors, then evaluate the bids and award the contract to your choice. The logic is that, everything being equal, you'll be able to select the best bid with the confidence that each contractor has interpreted your scope of work properly and been realistic about estimates and schedules.

The problem is that no two contractors bid alike, which sometimes can make their estimates difficult to compare. This is one reason I recommend hiring a restoration consultant, who can assist you in preparing the bid materials (blueprints and specifications) and reviewing the estimates to choose the right one. The three-bid rule also can put a premium on numbers, but I urge you to consider which of the bidding contractors you feel most comfortable with and can stand to see every day for the next several months. That consideration alone may steer you away from simply selecting the lowest bid, which is not always the best one.

An alternative to the three-bid rule is the negotiated contract. Instead of soliciting bids from three contractors, you take an extra step — interviewing — to narrow your list to just one contractor with whom you will refine the scope of work, establish terms and conditions for the project, set a schedule of completion and payments, and cement expectations for the job.

The interview stage allows the three or four contractors on your list to show their stuff, discuss projects similar to yours and offer creative ideas that may help lower your costs for the work and products you want (a practice called value engineering). Such meetings, typically no more than an hour long, also allow you to use your intuition about how your personalities will match up for what probably will be a long-term partnership.

In addition, interviews provide you the opportunity to scout the contractors' projects. Working through each contractor, obtain a list of recent clients and schedule walk-throughs, or tours, of their finished homes and works in progress. When touring jobs under construction, note specifically the condition of the site (inside and out), how materials are stored and waste eliminated. It's also a good idea to let each contractor walk you through to point out specific features or details that are similar to your project. If the homeowner is there, all the better; it will allow you to ask about the contractor's work habits, including adherence to schedule and budget and handling of subcontractors.

After meetings and scouting, it should become clear whom you want to hire as your contractor. While these steps take time and patience, they will allow you to decide on a contractor with infinitely more confidence than you would otherwise have. Your contractor will appreciate it, too, having gained insight into your approach, preparation and expectations.

Last, a few words about the contract itself. Many contractors offer a standard form, but important terms often are defined loosely or even omitted. My advice: draft one specific to your project with your selected contractor. Be as detailed as possible and include specifications, products, schedule, budget and payment due dates. Define responsibilities for liability, workers' compensation and other insurance; permits and inspections; lien releases and certificates; job site conditions; and the hiring of subcontractors. Preschedule periodic meetings and walk-throughs at critical points in the work.

As much as you hope to avoid butting heads during the job, the contract also should include agreed-upon procedures to resolve disputes. Dispute resolution can be as simple as agreeing to talk at the end of each work-day if communication becomes a problem, or it can include more legal procedures, such as arbitration or mediation, and who pays for legal fees, if any.

Being your own contractor   Managing a renovation project, especially a large-scale job, is a specialized skill. It requires full-time dedication, adherence to deadlines and budget, experience and savvy in politicking with local subcontractors, building inspectors and materials suppliers. It also demands a firm grasp of the construction process, attention to details — and vision.

Few homeowners are up to the task, nor should they expect themselves to be. Think you'll save money by managing the job yourself? No way.

Subcontractors and suppliers look upon owner-contractors as one-time jobs and frequently boost their prices to compensate for your assumed lack of experience. You'll also be in charge of the job flow and scheduling subcontractors, materials deliveries and inspections. Some building departments won't issue a permit unless you have a contractor's license, which means you'll have to get one of your subs to do it. You'll be expected to inspect the work, know what you're looking at and be able to defend it to a building inspector. Worst-case scenario: you may damage the historic character and features of your home and have to pay a bundle to a contractor to fix and finish what you couldn't.

In short, if your goal is to save money, it's not by being your own general contractor. If you want to be involved beyond project management, evaluate your handyman skills; if you enjoy nailing drywall, scraping wood siding, hauling debris, cleaning up after the crew has gone home or making a few runs to the wood refinisher, you perhaps cansave yourself a few thousand dollars. Or, spend your time visiting salvage yards, hardware stores and garage sales to pick up items and refinish them, and let the professionals handle the big stuff.

the right tools

This book assumes that you'll hire professionals to do the bulk of the **restoration and preservation** work on your older home, and I hope I've convinced you of the wisdom of making that choice for yourself. But proper and periodic maintenance of a home includes several tasks you can do — with the right tools.

Using the right tool is the key to success with any job, from fixing fence rails to touching up paint. A lot of time, hard-earned experience and a fair share of science has gone into the development of tools for carpentry and home repair; just take a look at the tool table at any salvage shop or garage sale and you'll find tools with funky handles and heads of various shapes and contours designed for specific, if outdated, purposes.

Today's tools are more sophisticated, if no less specifically designed for given tasks. Electric, pneumatic (air pressure–driven) and cordless tools have by and large replaced hand tools for many jobs. They are designed to make various carpentry and construction projects easier, faster and safer.

With few exceptions, however, these tools are overkill for homeowners with some skills and an interest in taking a hands-on role in the preservation of their restored historic home.

If you're like me, though, you take one look at the tool aisles and racks at the local hardware store and begin to drool. My advice (if not my actual practice) is to start slow, gather the essentials and add to them as needed. A basic tool set is essential — and affordable. You can purchase that pickax and circular saw down the road, but for now you just need the basics.

Whether they're wire cutters in your hand, a belt full of hammers, chisels, screwdrivers and tape measures or just a strong stepladder upon which to stand, the right tools make every job easier.

Start with a 16-inch toolbox with a lift-out tray; I prefer metal, but hard plastic is okay and, while not as sturdy, is lighter. These boxes provide plenty of room for the basic set of tools yet are small enough to fit just about anywhere; always keep yours accessible, and, as a rule, always return your tools to the box after you have finished using them.

Now, add a 13-to-16-ounce claw-style hammer, which is heavy enough for banging nails yet light enough to control easily when affixing a picture hook to the wall. One flat and one Phillips screwdriver, both of medium head size, will work for most screws around the house. I usually hesitate to recommend universal screwdrivers, which come with several interchangeable bits (or heads), if only because the bits can come loose during use and also are easily lost.

Next comes a 16-foot retractable, metal tape measure, which is long and sturdy enough to measure most room dimensions and ceiling heights without becoming unwieldy. Finally, add a pair of 5- and 10-inch vise grips, which hold things in place and also can be used for light plumbing jobs, like turning off valves or removing shower heads. I also would throw in a set of clear-plastic safety goggles and a pair of light-duty gloves. Grand total for the whole set: about $75.

Other fun, useful tools include a battery-powered stud finder, which helps locate the structural framing behind plaster to best secure fasteners and picture hangers (though in truly historic renovations, using a picture mold to hang artwork is more accurate). A professional-grade cordless screwdriver or drill motor with a full set of bits and an extender will provide the necessary torque to remove stubborn screws (don't ditch your hand drivers, though, because they often can sneak into spaces too tight for a drill motor). And while they won't fit in your toolbox, no home should be without a 24-foot extension ladder and a step stool for hanging Christmas lights, checking out the gutters and safely lifting boxes to or from a high shelf in the storage closet or yard shed.

Finally, don't forget to throw in a video or book telling you everything you need to know about restoring older homes (though I can't imagine where you'd find either…), and you're set.

Like your home, your tools also need maintenance for peak performance; keep them clean and stored in a dry, temperate place and replace broken handles and chipped blades, as necessary. And, please, always think safety first with any task; wear your goggles and gloves, have someone hold the ladder, and work with plenty of light and ventilation to avoid accidents and injury.

Garden and yard tools Your landscape and other yard and garden features will determine the specific tools you'll need to maintain the outside property, but there are a few basic items that every home should have.

Among the essentials are a good, wide leaf rake and a sturdy garden rake for gravel areas and larger debris, a spade and a shovel, a few garden trowels for close-in work, and pruning shears and clippers. I also recommend a tree pruner, preferably one that extends to 15 feet or so, to make seasonal or ad-hoc repairs to overgrown, broken or dead tree branches. As with tools for carpentry, be sure your yard equipment is kept sharp, clean and in good repair; doing so will make every job easier and safer.

If gardening is one of your passions (but hauling lawn clippings and pruned branches isn't), I'd also consider a mulching mower, which plows clippings back into the turf, providing your lawn with nutrients naturally. If you have a lot of shrubs and small trees that need periodic pruning, also consider a chipper. Not only does it make the task less labor intensive, but chipped branches can be stored in a trash barrel (a 20-gallon, heavy-plastic bin with handles and a lid will suffice) and reused as mulch and weed control around shrubs and other plantings. Perhaps most important, these two pieces of equipment save landfill space.

It bears repeating that safety should be top of mind when tackling any yard or garden project, whether it requires motorized or hand-held cutting equipment. (Ironically, part of good safety is keeping the blades of these tools sharp.) I'd also stress wearing safety goggles, working on a sturdy platform or level base and taking frequent breaks to rest your muscles and your tools.

Renting tools Several maintenance jobs around the house and yard require special tools that simply aren't used often enough to justify the purchase price. Extralong (36-foot) extension ladders, paint sprayers, gas-powered augers and trenchers for fence and deck postholes and watering systems, compressors, hoses and equipment for pneumatic tools, among others, fit this category.

However, all of these and more are available from local rental outlets. For a small deposit (or just your credit card number on file) and a show of picture identification, you can walk out with tools you'd never dreamed existed — or that you actually would get to use. They typically are kept in great condition, tuned regularly and run at peak efficiency. The folks behind the counter can help you with on-the-job safety advice, maintenance requirements (adding oil and cleaning) and troubleshooting, not to mention the proper use of the tool and what you can expect it to do. Return it in like condition and you won't suffer losing your deposit or incurring extra charges.

If you repeatedly find yourself going back to the rental house for the same tool or piece of equipment, such as a chain saw or rototiller, consider partnering with a neighbor or neighborhood group to purchase one new and share it. A community I know of near Seattle shares and maintains all their lawn and garden equipment. To be sure, it has saved them money; more important, it has built friendships and allowed them to share the load.

Even if you use a professional carpenter or contractor to perform the major work on your renovation or restoration, there will be lots of leftover chores for you to do. Good tools and a home workshop make the job easier and more fun.

This simple home workshop provides all necessary and basic equipment for safe and convenient repair and construction in the typical home. Besides plumbing and carpentry tools, it includes storage space, safety and first aid equipment.

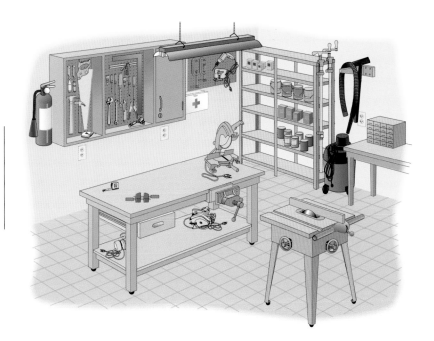

about health & safety

Restoring older homes has grown from a cottage culture in a few sleepy towns to a nationwide, multimillion-dollar industry. Among the by-products of this growth is an **increased commitment** to eliminating safely such environmental hazards as lead-based paint, carbon monoxide, asbestos and radon gas that might be discovered in the process. These four elements are potential killers, not to be taken lightly or handled carelessly. They also are not limited to older homes, so it is important to get all the facts before you take any measures. Professional abatement and service contractors are available to inspect your home for such exposure, address options and costs, and seal, remove or repair any problems. An inspection is a must if you are considering the purchase of an older home, even if you don't plan to renovate it.

Safety in renovation projects requires attention to two factors: hazards encountered because of the work and the practices used to perform the work. Use a helper.

Lead-based paint Until the mid-1970s, lead was an ingredient in both exterior- and interior-grade paints because it added durability. It mostly was used on homes built before 1950, although if your home was constructed in the '60s or '70s, your interior surfaces should be checked.

The danger with lead-based paint lies in the dust, chips or flakes — from peeling or being removed from walls, window sills or other surfaces being ingested by children or pets. The ingestion of lead-based paint poisons the bloodstream; in fact, the Center for Disease Control lists it as the leading health threat to today's

children. However, public awareness of its hazards and commonsense practices in its removal (as well as regulations against leaded gasoline, another lead hazard) have reduced the number of cases significantly.

There are a few ways to test for lead in the painted surfaces of your home. The easiest is a swipe test, which is available at your local hardware store or home center. A treated swab is put to the painted area; if it turns red, lead is present in the paint or on the surface. If by chance the paint you're testing is red (thereby making the red indicator on the swab hard to read), there are alternative swipe tests, albeit with more toxic active ingredients, to detect the presence of lead. These tests are not as commonly used and might be available only from lead abatement contractors.

To test for lead below a surface, professional technicians can conduct an X-ray fluorescent (XRF) test, which can detect lead through some 20 layers of paint. (This test detects the presence of lead and analyzes its concentration.) An XRF test can run a few hundred dollars or more depending on the amount of area tested, but is well worth it if peace of mind is in question.

To remove paint that contains lead mechanically or manually (such as on your clapboard siding), first make sure the paint surface is dampened. That way, the chips will fall onto a disposable tarp or other ground cover rather than create a dust than can be inhaled; nevertheless, always wear a double-filtered respirator with filter cartridges rated for lead dust. When removing paint mechanically, make sure the sander/scraper is hooked directly to a shop vacuum to collect the chips and dust for disposal.

Whichever method you choose, contact your local hazardous materials agency to dispose properly of the paint chips. [For manual paint removal from wood surfaces, see chapters Two and Three.]

If you want more information about lead-based paint and its hazards, I recommend a free video/brochure package available from the Iowa Department of Public Health [(800) 972-2026], as well as materials from a resource called Lead Smart (best reached on the World Wide Web at www.leadsmarthomes.com), which offers a video, CD-ROM and diskette package covering lead-based paint issues; the cost depends on the package you purchase.

Carbon monoxide You've no doubt heard news stories about families dying in their sleep from high levels of carbon monoxide (CO) in their homes. These tragedies are rare, but they do signal a general concern for the presence of CO in homes nationwide.

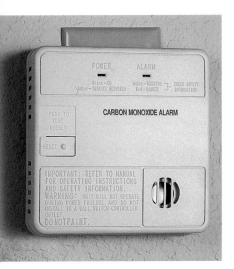

Ceiling-mounted carbon monoxide detectors are inexpensive and effective.

Carbon monoxide is created by the combustion of fuel — natural gas, wood, coal or oil — used to power various household appliances, HVAC equipment and fireplaces. It is a colorless, odorless, toxic gas that, upon entering the lungs, reduces the amount of oxygen carried to the bloodstream. Symptoms of CO poisoning range from headaches and nausea to fainting and loss of consciousness.

If you suspect the presence of CO in your house, first look to your gas furnace and water heater and their ventilation systems. Improperly sized flues or those with cracks or blockage can allow CO gasses to vent back into rooms rather than to the outside; one red flag is if your pilot light burns low and yellow.

Untended chimneys — cracked, without a flue liner or partially blocked by nests, soot or other debris — also can redirect carbon monoxide to the interior. A telltale sign of a chimney that has the potential to or already may allow CO infiltration is one with black stains or dampness on the exterior, the by-product of soot (or creosote) buildup inside the vent.

Finally, unless properly and periodically maintained, fuel-burning appliances can emit carbon monoxide into your home's rooms. Efforts to tighten your home against heat loss, such as caulking and weatherstripping, may serve only to trap the gas, preventing its proper ventilation.

To protect yourself and your family, have your entire heating and ventilating system, and your fireplace and chimney, professionally inspected and cleaned before the start of each heating season. You may have to add to your ducting or update your ventilation system, replace filters or flue liners, or install air cleaners to ventilate the indoor air properly. Any blockage or buildup anywhere in your system can cause a CO hazard, so regular, thorough maintenance is well worth whatever amount it costs.

You also may want to install carbon monoxide detectors, which are similar to smoke detectors in appearance and operation. Place one in each bedroom and in all common areas, taking care not to put them too close to combustion appliances such as the furnace or water heater, which may emit short bursts of carbon monoxide on start-up and set off the alarm. And, be sure to install CO detectors in the ceiling (where the gas is likely to flow with the warm, heated air) to keep them out of the reach of children and pets.

If you've taken these measures but still are concerned, I recommend hiring a professional to conduct an air test, in which an electric pump forces the indoor air through a series of filters, then is taken to a lab for analysis. For other tips on CO abatement, contact your local office of the Environmental Protection Agency, or dial up www.homesafe.com/coalert on the World Wide Web.

Asbestos As insulating material, few are better than asbestos. However, as an environmental and health hazard, few are worse. Determined to be carcinogenic in the 1970s, asbestos was phased out quickly as a component of insulation and other products, such as floor and ceiling tiles. So, in homes built before then, asbestos (like lead-based paint) still may be present.

In older homes, asbestos is commonly found as insulation for exposed plumbing pipes, in kitchen floor tiles and other applications. As it deteriorates, asbestos becomes friable (or loose), creating airborne particles than can be inhaled into the lungs. The solution is to seal or cover any asbestos-based products before it becomes friable.

If an asbestos-based product isn't chipping or flaking (meaning the asbestos has not become friable yet), the simplest, most effective way to protect your family from its effects is to trap and encapsulate it — on the ceiling, with paint; on the floor, with another covering whose adhesives will prevent the asbestos from becoming loose and airborne. If asbestos-based insulation applied to pipes has not become friable, you can paint it or cover it with a foam sheath with confidence that it has done the job.

Removal of friable asbestos should be left to professionals, period. For a free brochure on asbestos and its warning signs, call or contact the U.S. Consumer Product Safety Commission in Washington, D.C., at (202) 554-1404.

Radon Radon is a colorless, odorless gas that escapes from rock formations and soils in certain areas of the country, especially during excavation but also at other times in locations where it is common, and can invade your house. Unlike carbon monoxide, there are no immediate or recognizable symptoms of radon gas presence; however, studies have determined it to be carcinogenic, and the effects may not show up for decades.

Definitively diagnosing the presence or absence of radon can take up to a year because the home should undergo seasonal changes to get a range of exposures. The most reliable test is a carbon strip, placed in the basement or lowest level of the home, then lab tested; canister tests, though common and also lab tested, are short-term indicators at best.

If radon is detected to be higher than 4 picocurries per liter of air (the EPA's benchmark for a safe level), there are four ways to solve the problem: filtration, dilution, redirection and source control. Each is effective, depending on the situation and space and budget limitations. In rare cases, the source of the radon infiltration and the extent of the problem may require mitigation, the cost of which can run into the thousands of dollars.

Filtration typically involves adding an appliance, like an air cleaner, to vent and filter the radon gas from the indoor air to the outside, where it safely dissipates. The downsides are a potential increase in your energy bill and periodic maintenance of another appliance.

Dilution often is more effective and less costly. Venting your basement or crawl space simply by opening a window and adding a fan will force the radon gas to dissipate safely to the outdoors. The downside, again, may be a slight increase in your energy costs.

Redirection requires finding the precise entry (or entries) of the gas and passively or forcibly directing it out-doors. Many older homes have sump pits and pumps in their basements or crawl spaces to prevent damage to the home during a flood. However, sump pits often are points of radon entry. To seal and vent them against radon, yet retain their effectiveness during a flood, run a 4-inch ABS or PVC pipe to a sidewall or through the roof (using an existing chase) and add a continuously running fan, if necessary, to ensure a constant outward flow of air. Do not even consider sealing the pump; the indoor air pressure simply will force the gas to enter in another place, such as cracks in the basement slab or below-grade walls, and meanwhile you will have rendered the sump useless.

Ultimately, you'll want to find and correct the source of radon entry, whether it be sealing cracks in the basement floor and along below-grade walls or complex excavation and installation of drain tiles. Whatever you or a professional does, you'll want to avoid disturbing or harming any historical features of your home and its yard and landscape.

General health and safety Building codes are established to regulate health and safety, and licensed contractors often are required by contract or law to carry liability and workers' compensation insurance. But it ultimately is your responsibility to ensure the health and safety of yourself and your family during a restoration project.

As you begin working with your contractor, discuss how construction zones will be cordoned off to limit traffic from family members and pets, how and where materials and power tools will be stored, if there is adequate electrical service for the crew's equipment and what arrangements are needed for trash disposal. Even if you and your contractor have agreed on all these issues, know that you probably will be the one liable for damage to an adjacent tree or yard, any street or curb scars or injuries to neighborhood kids climbing on the dumpster.

Another general safety consideration concerns electric, phone and gas lines. Naturally, such lines pose a significant hazard from shock and explosion in the event of an accident. Most utility companies prefer that you or your contractor contact them before working near their overhead or underground power and gas lines — a preference they usually enforce by holding you liable for any damage, even if it was accidental.

The hazards of any job site are too many to detail in a short appendix, but the following are the ones of most concern.

First, there is construction waste: it's a tripping hazard as well as the source of such nasty surprises as nails, sharp bits of old metal flashing and broken tile or glass. Set aside a few minutes at the end of each shift for cleanup — stacking and piling dangerous waste, pulling nails from discarded lumber or, better yet, making sure it all makes its way into the dumpster.

Another key hazard: the job site itself. Open balcony railings, empty stairwells, pits, holes and obstacles make the place a booby trap for the unwary. A little construction safety tape can help make the hazards clearer. Many novices wonder why windows and sliding doors are delivered with those hard-to-remove stickers and wax markings all over their surfaces. The reason couldn't be a better one — I can't tell you how many times I've seen people walk into a door or window that wasn't there a few hours earlier!

Next, there are the power tools. A rotary saw with no blade guard — or one whose absence was ignored during a critical cut — has sent more than one carpenter to the emergency room. Drills can penetrate clothing and body parts as easily as they do wood and concrete. Power planers and air-driven tools can slice, dice and send slivers flying at unbelievable speeds. Keep these potential hazards safe by showing them proper respect — and by keeping children off the project site.

Finally, make sure the project area is secured at night: I use a sheet of plywood nailed into place to block temporary openings. Despite this, passersby sometimes do find their way inside. If theft is a concern, make sure valuable tools and materials either are stored safely or removed from the job site.

Never forget: tired hands and heads make anyone careless, but some steps in every project must be completed at a single run. Concrete pours are just one example — curing concrete waits for no man. When a critical section must be finished at the end of a long shift, stress that extra care be taken.

Many insurance companies offer temporary liability policies for large-scale construction projects, such as a whole-house restoration. Check them out.

Also, if you plan to do any work yourself, make sure you have the proper equipment — good-quality work goggles should be worn for any kind of cutting; dust masks for airborne debris, including fiberglass insulation, paint and sawdust; and gloves, always. When transporting heavy materials, consider wearing steel-toed safety shoes or boots. Finally, no job site (or household, for that matter) should be without a well-stocked first aid kit.

ABS — Black, rigid plastic, typically used for piping.

Adaptive reuse — Converting a building originally intended for one use, such as a carriage house, to another use, such as living space.

Aerating — The process of poking holes in turf to facilitate deeper penetration of water and nutrients to the roots and to loosen compacted soil.

Balloon frame — A structural framing technique in which vertical posts and studs extend from the sill plate at the foundation to the top plate at the roof eaves, creating a continuous path for structural loads.

Bays — Sections of fencing between posts.

Below grade — Under the natural or excavated ground level.

Bids — Estimated costs to perform construction work.

Brown coat — The second, or base, coat of plaster or stucco.

Bump-outs — On the exterior of a house, the architectural details that extend from the basic structure of the house, such as bay windows, cantilevered window seats, balconies and dormers, etc.

Casement window — A window that swings out as a single unit.

Casing — The frame of a door.

Cedar shakes — The untapered, thicker brethren of cedar shingles.

Chalking — On aluminum siding, what happens when the finish and coating deteriorate to a fine powder you can rub off with your hand.

Closed flashing — A flashing technique that weaves the roof shingles to create a seamless appearance (also called woven or cut).

Comp roofing — Industry term for asphalt composition shingles.

Comps — A term in the home appraisal business referring to homes of like size, age, design and number of rooms. A comparison or comparable home.

Conduits — In electrical wiring, flexible metal piping that houses and protects bundles of wires.

Control joints — In a monolithic concrete slab, strategically placed joints tooled into the surface to which cracks will gravitate, keeping the main surface clear.

Cricket or saddle — A roof flashing technique to shed water away from the backside of a chimney.

Crimp — The molded detail that interlocks panels of a standing seam metal roof.

Crown — A natural or molded curvature that helps shed water away from the surface, usually concrete. Structural lumber may also have a crown, or curvature, along its length.

Cured — Dry, as in cured concrete or cured plaster.

Decking — The platform created by roof or floor sheathing, or boards on an exterior deck structure.

Designer shingle — An asphalt composition shingle on which the granules are arranged to simulate a shadow, color, texture or other dimensional effect.

Disking — Turning over dead patches of grass for reseeding; also called tilling.

Dovetail — In finish carpentry, a molded joint wider at its end than at its base that interlocks with an adjacent groove.

Drip edge — A metal piece of flashing that extends along the roof eaves and sheds water from the shingles to the sidewalls, preventing it from running underneath the eaves and the shingles.

Efflorescence — The leaching of salts through masonry and mortar.

Facade — The front elevation of a building.

Fascia — The front portion of the roof structure, at or under the eaves.

Feather — Surfaces that are lightly sanded to create a seamless connection with other materials or finishes.

Fly-by-night — A term for unscrupulous or dishonest contractors who do not complete a job on time or within budget.

Frost line — The depth at which the ground freezes in your area.

Galvanized — Zinc-coated steel or other metal, typically found as roofing material, plumbing pipes or nails.

Grade — Ground level.

Grading the surface — Excavation or other preparation of a surface, typically the building pad or site.

Hardboard siding — Engineered or composite wood panels that resemble solid or sawn wood but are made from compressed wood fibers or paper, adhesives, wax and other binders.

Hardscapes — Paved areas in a landscaping plan or design.

Hewn — Shaped, typically by hand or with a hand tool.

Insulated glass — Two panels of glass separated by air and sealed together, providing additional insulating qualities.

Joint — Where two materials intersect or overlap.

Keying — Plaster or stucco compounds pressed between the slats of the lath; when dry, the keys hold the plaster or stucco to the structural wall.

Lath — Narrow strips of wood laid parallel to one another and nailed to the stud wall or ceiling, over which plaster is applied and to which it structurally adheres.

Lien — A legally binding claim for compensation of materials and labor provided to a project by a contractor; it must be settled via lien releases, certificates or waivers (i.e., the contractor is paid according to the agreement) prior to obtaining clear title to the property.

Life-cycle costs — An analysis of a material's or system's cost to purchase, install, operate and maintain over a period of time (the longer, the better).

Linoleum — An organic, durable combination of linseed oil, rosin, wood flour, cork powder, natural pigments and mildew inhibitors over a jute, canvas or felt backing; the precursor to vinyl flooring and laminate coverings on countertops.

Low-flow toilet — Toilets that use less than 3.5 gallons of water per flush.

Mill finish — Uncoated; typically refers to aluminum roofing or flashing.

Mud jacking — A technique in which a concrete slurry is pumped underneath a paved area (driveway or walkway) through holes drilled in the surface to lift a section of concrete level with other sections.

Open flashing — A flashing technique in which a continuous, molded piece of metal is installed between the roofing material and the area being protected from water runoff.

Outbuildings — Detached buildings, such as sheds or gazebos.

Pans — Metal roofing panels that extend from ridge to eaves as a continuous piece.

Patina — A fine greenish crust on bronze or copper created by oxidation.

Platform framing — A structural framing technique in which the vertical members extend only to the next floor or level.

Precut running mold — A shaped hand tool for the creation of plaster moldings and details.

Pull permits — The process of applying for and being issued a building permit by the local building department.

Punch list — The last remaining items to be completed.

PVC — White, rigid plastic, typically used for piping.

Rafters — The primary structural members of the roof frame.

Raised panel — A molded or crafted panel set loosely into a door frame, allowing the wood to naturally expand and contract to changes in climate yet maintain the structural integrity of the door itself.

Reglazing — A process of replacing putty that holds the window glass to its frame.

Replacement siding — A generic term for any siding material, typically aluminum or vinyl, that is used to cover up or replace a home's existing wood or masonry siding.

Repointing — Refilling or replacing mortar between bricks or concrete blocks.

Ridge vent — A continuous vent along the topmost edge (or ridge) of the roof, which circulates stuffy air out of the attic along the roof's peak. A ridge vent works in conjunction with eaves or soffit vents.

Ring-shank nails — Fasteners with threads of raised rings along their length, typically for roofing.

Runoff — Rain or melting snow shedding off the roof, sidewalls or paved areas.

Sash windows — Also called hung windows; refers to window sections that open and close horizontally within the frame.

Scabbing — See *"Sistering."*

Scab-ons — Structural additions that do not match the existing character, forms, materials or mass of the original building. An out-of-place or -scale addition.

Scalping — Overcutting grass blades, which then may turn yellow.

Scarfing — To splice a new section in place of a damaged area.

Scope of work — A detailed, mutually agreed-upon, step-by-step description of the work to be done.

Scouting — Visiting restoration projects under construction or completed to gather ideas, observe conditions and solicit contractor referrals.

Scratch coat — The first coat of plaster or stucco, on which the surface is scratched up to better adhere to the second (or brown) coat.

Sheathing — Boards or panels that are nailed to the roof and wall framing for structural stability and to act as the substrate or surface for roofing or siding materials. Typically 4x8-foot sheets of plywood or other insulating structural material of like dimension.

Shingle course — A row of shingles on the roof or sidewall.

Shiplap — A method for connecting wood planks, typically flooring or exterior siding, in which the adjoining edges overlap.

Shoring — Temporary support of a load-bearing structural member or section.

Sill plate — The horizontal section that rests on top of the foundation and holds the vertical wall studs.

Sistering — Attaching a new section to the original material, typically structural lumber, to reinforce it along its length. Also called scabbing.

Snow jacks — On a metal roof, slight metal projections that help snow grip the roof surface.

Soffit — The underside of the rafters or the eaves.

Spaced sheathing — On the roof, strips of wood set perpendicular to the rafters (roof framing) to create a ladderlike pattern for the installation of cedar shingles. The gaps between the slats ventilate the shingles from underneath, helping them dry out after rain or snow.

Specifications — A detailed, mutually agreed-upon list of materials to be ordered or purchased, including brand names, model numbers, colors, finishes and other details.

Splash block — A tapered and sloped concrete or plastic block positioned at the end of a downspout or extender to further disperse water runoff from the foundation.

Spline-and-groove connectors — Wood flooring planks connected by concealed splines inset into grooves on the under-side of the planks.

Square — A roofing term to define an area measuring 10x10 feet, or 100 square feet.

Square-butt — Edges that align across a surface, typically on a three-tab asphalt composition roof shingle.

Standing seam — A roofing system of interlocking panels, typically metal.

Starter course — The first row of shingles on a roof or sidewall.

Step flashing — Single pieces of metal bent to the proper angle and slope installed along both sides of intersecting vertical walls; named for how the metal pieces are stepped up the slope of the walls to shed water.

Subs — Subcontractors or specialty trades-people, such as plumbers, electricians and plasterers.

Substrate — An underlying material hidden beneath a surface, such as subfloor beneath ceramic tile or wallboard under paint or wallpaper.

Terne — A tin/lead coating over an iron base used as a roofing or flashing material.

Three-tab — A style of asphalt composition roofing in which the shingle panel is separated into three sections by slender notches to add dimension and help drain water away from the shingles.

Tongue-and-groove — A method for connecting wood planks, typically flooring or exterior siding, in which one of the adjoining edges is molded with a projecting rib that fits into a molded groove on the other adjoining edge.

Tooling — The removal of excess moisture and mortar from a brick or concrete block structure to create a waterproof seal.

Valley — On the roof, where the downside of two pitches intersect, creating a gutter to the eaves.

Vapor barrier — Typically, plastic sheeting installed on the "warm" side of a wall, floor or ceiling between the structural framing and the sheathing or finish material to block moisture from entering the cavity and condensing against the "cold" side. Some paints and interior decorative panels can serve as a vapor barrier.

Veneer — A thin sheet or covering over a substrate material.

Vignette — A display in a kitchen or bath showroom or home center.

Wallboard — A construction panel made of gypsum or a similar filler sandwiched between two outer coverings of building paper. Also called drywall and Sheetrock™, it is commonly used in place of plaster for interior wall finishes.

Walk-through — An inspection of the home prior to closing escrow.

Xeriscaping — A landscaping method utilizing plantings and soils that conserve water naturally or rely on an area's seasonal and annual rainfall for their sole source of water.

index

credits

Photograph on page vii by Raul Cabra/courtesy Cabra Diseño.

Photographs on pages ii (bottom), 2 (right), 5 (both), 17 (center), 20 (left), 21, 26 (top), 69, 74, 85, 89, 90 (top), 91, 93, 94 (top), 95, 98 (bottom), 102, 107, 111 (bottom), 112, 124, 129, 132 (right), 139, 142 (middle) and 147 (top) by Alan Copeland.

Photographs on pages vi (bottom), 70 (right), 71, 84, 119 and 126 (both) by Doug Dealey.

Photographs on pages ii (top), 24 (both), 40 (bottom) and 149 by Robert Dolezal.

Photographs on pages 8–9, 12–13 by Dwight Young/courtesy National Trust for Historic Preservation.

Photograph on page 4 courtesy National Trust for Historic Preservation.

Photographs on pages vi (top), 1, 3, 6 (both), 7 (all), 11 (both), 16 (all), 17 (top left and right, and bottom), 19, 25, 26 (bottom), 27, 28 (both), 31, 33 (both), 35, 37, 39 (both), 38, 40 (top and middle), 41 (all), 43, 46, 48, 49, 51, 52–53, 55, 56–57 (all), 76, 77 (both), 78 (bottom), 79, 80, 90 (bottom), 92, 94 (bottom), 96, 97, 98 (top), 100, 104, 105, 108 (right), 110 (all), 111 (top), 113, 114, 116 (both), 121, 123, 125 (both), 127, 131, 136, 138, 141, 142 (top and bottom), 143 (all), 145 (both), 147 (bottom), 157 and 164 by John M. Rickard.

All photographs of Bob Yapp on the cover, and on pages x, 2 (left), 20 (right), 70 (left), 94 (center), 108 (left), 132 (left), 152, 158 and 162, by Michael J. Winter/The Chicago Production Center, used by permission of WTTW.

The publisher gratefully acknowledges SC Johnson Wax for its cooperation regarding the photographs that taken at The Johnson Homestead and used in this book. We also gratefully acknowledge the cooperation of the following individuals, companies and groups for their assistance during production, photography and illustration: James B. Clapp, Louise Davis, Becky Powell, John S. Rickard, John Tepley; Kitchen Design Center, Ohmega Salvage, Ray's Electrical and Plumbing Supply, Silmar Flooring, Tile Town and Yorkshire Roofing; and the employees of the Robert Yapp Company.

Production of the public television series

About Your House with Bob Yapp

is made possible by the generous support

of these organizations:

Ace is the place with the helpful hardware folks.

www.acehardware.com
(630) 990-6600

www.andersenwindows.com
(800) 426-4261 x 1232

THE PAST BUILDS THE FUTURE.

www.nationaltrust.org
(800) 944-NTHP